WHEN THE KING COMES BACK

These Books by
OSWALD J. SMITH

Uniform in style

THE DAY OF SALVATION
THE CHALLENGE OF LIFE
THE MARVELS OF GRACE
PROPHECY: WHAT LIES AHEAD?
THE MAN GOD USES
THE WORK GOD BLESSES
THE REVIVAL WE NEED
THE ENDUEMENT OF POWER
THE COUNTRY I LOVE BEST
THE SPIRIT AT WORK
THE VOICE OF PROPHECY
THE GOSPEL WE PREACH
DAVID BRAINERD
THE PASSION FOR SOULS
BATTLE FOR TRUTH
THE THINGS WE KNOW
WHEN THE KING COMES BACK
THE CONSUMING FIRE
THE ADVENTURES OF ANDY MCGINNIS
THE STORIES OF THOMAS

Marshall, Morgan & Scott, Ltd.
London :: Edinburgh

WHEN THE KING COMES BACK

by

OSWALD J. SMITH, Litt.D.

(*Pastor of The Peoples Church, Toronto*)

Introduction by

WILBUR M. SMITH, D.D.

*Professor of English Bible, Fuller Theological Seminary
Editor of Peloubet's Select Notes on The International
Sunday School Lessons*

D. Edmond Hiebert

London
MARSHALL, MORGAN & SCOTT
Edinburgh

LONDON
MARSHALL, MORGAN AND SCOTT, LTD.
33 LUDGATE HILL, E.C.4

AUSTRALIA
317 COLLINS STREET
MELBOURNE

NEW ZEALAND
23 MONTGOMERY ROAD
ROTHESAY BAY
AUCKLAND

SOUTH AFRICA
P.O. BOX 1720, STURK'S BUILDINGS
CAPE TOWN

CANADA
EVANGELICAL PUBLISHERS
366 BAY STREET
TORONTO

THE PEOPLES PRESS
100 BLOOR EAST
TORONTO

U.S.A.
WORLD LITERATURE CRUSADE PRESS
BOX 1313, STUDIO CITY
CALIFORNIA

This edition 1957

MADE AND PRINTED IN GREAT BRITAIN BY PURNELL AND SONS, LTD.
PAULTON (SOMERSET) AND LONDON

INTRODUCTION

By Dr. Wilbur M. Smith

Professor of English Bible, Fuller Theological Seminary, Pasadena, California; Editor of Peloubet's Select Notes on the International Sunday School Lessons.

FOR VARIOUS REASONS, books on prophetic subjects are pouring from the presses of England and the United States more frequently than ever before. If one includes all the subjects of biblical prophecy, the Second Advent of Christ, the kingdom of God, eschatology, and books treating of the future from a somewhat secular standpoint, I believe he will find that a new book in this area now appears every thirty-six hours. In addition to these, there are innumerable periodical articles being published, some of them of great importance. Works on biblical eschatology are being written by four different groups of men.

First of all, there is the group which writes from a standpoint of severe critical scholarship, interested in the more profound theological implications of eschatology, and taking into account the latest

INTRODUCTION

theories of both Old and New Testament criticism. This group would include Barth, Brunner, Bultmann, Dibelius, and many others. Whatever the conclusions of these authors might be, their writings are exercising a great influence in the thought of Western Christendom today. Dr. Smith makes no pretence of writing from this viewpoint.

At the other extreme are those who write to defend or expound the fantastic eschatological views of many of our modern cults, such as the Anglo-Israelites, Jehovah's Witnesses, the Church of the Latter-Day Saints, and many smaller circles of self-styled students of prophecy. However wide be the contemporary influence of these writers, their books are ephemeral, and the sequence of historical events compel constant revisions and frequent apologies. This type of literature can be ignored.

A third group writing on prophetic subjects is made up of men who, though passing by what might be called the critical problems of biblical investigation, have given their lives to the careful, reverent study of the prophetic Scriptures, and who prayerfully and carefully attempt to set forth what the Word of God has to say regarding certain aspects of the future, concerning which, after all, we have no certainty apart from what is revealed in the Holy Scriptures. Among these would be Ironside, Haldeman, G. H. Lang, Panton, etc., etc.

INTRODUCTION

Finally, there is a fourth group, not exactly synonymous with the third, though certain individuals may be found in both, composed of that small band of outstanding leaders of evangelical Christianity, who, through many years of abundantly fruitful ministry, of nights of prayer, and weeks and months of preaching, through their great passion for missions, and intimate knowledge of world conditions, are able to express mature convictions regarding the significance of the prophetic Scriptures. My beloved friend, the author of this small book now offered to the public, certainly belongs in *both* of these last-named classifications of writers.

One will read this volume with far greater interest if he has some preliminary knowledge of the author. Dr. Oswald J. Smith, born in 1889, has produced this volume after reaching the age of sixty, and, what is more, after preaching the Gospel with power over a period of forty-six years, beginning when eighteen years of age. He comes to the study of the Word of God with full equipment. He not only attended lectures in the Toronto Bible College and other institutes of biblical training in North America, but was graduated from McCormick Theological Seminary, being a minister of the Presbyterian Church of Canada.

While many who are gifted in writing and in the interpretation of the Scriptures have never ministered

INTRODUCTION

to large congregations, and, I think, need not apologize for this, the author of this book has had a ministry identified with large audiences from the time he was a young man preaching in Chicago, and then in Los Angeles; in fact, it is commonly understood that the church which he served as pastor in Los Angeles—I need not give the name here—near the beginning of our century, has never since experienced the life, and attendance, which it knew under the leadership of this young minister.

Since 1930, he has been the well-known pastor of The Peoples Church, Toronto, Canada. The auditorium accommodates some two thousand people, and there is rarely a Sunday that it is not filled to capacity at both morning and evening services, except during July and August, an unusual phenomenon in our day, especially north of the Mason-Dixon Line (and something not too frequently seen even in the "Bible Belt"). Here in California, I often drive by churches which, though they have two or three thousand members on their respective rolls, have neither a Sunday evening service nor a prayer meeting, from January to December, year after year!

To preach for a quarter of a century to a congregation like Dr. Smith's would be enough for most men in a lifetime, but not for him, who, with a burning passion for the proclamation of the Gospel

INTRODUCTION

throughout the world, has made nine world tours to visit the mission stations of our globe, and has a church which now gives nearly three hundred thousand dollars annually to missions, and which participates in the support of over three hundred and fifty missionaries. The correspondence alone for this kind of work must be enormous.

Probably no man living in North America today, still active in the Christian ministry, has brought inspiration and vision to as many men and women concerning the missionary obligation resting upon the Church of Christ as Dr. Oswald Smith. Some years ago my friend, Dr. Harold J. Ockenga, told me that his own great missionary programme became the powerful, dominating factor in their church through the annual visits of Dr. Smith to lead the missionary conferences at Park Street Church in Boston.

In addition to his preaching, his world tours, and his missionary activities, Dr. Smith has had time, energy, and vision for writing twenty books, and over six hundred hymns, poems, and Gospel songs. There is probably no song book, for general use in church and Sunday School, being published today, that does not include one or more of these hymns, some of which will be used until our Lord returns. I need not go into a discussion of them in this brief prefatory word. How many hundreds of

INTRODUCTION

thousands of people have been blessed and inspired by the author's writings, I do not know.

Personally, I shall never forget when, as a pastor in Covington, Virginia, a copy of his book, *The Work God Blesses*, fell into my hands. I could not get away from it for months and months after reading it, as also his work, *The Revival We Need*. My only regret is that the deep effect that these books have had upon me has not resulted in a far greater evangelistic ministry during my own lifetime.

It is not my purpose here to try to discover the secret of a life of such abundant ministry. In reading his autobiography, *The Story of My Life*, however, I came upon one experience after another, from the time he was a young man down to these later years, in which, on his knees before God, he would dedicate and rededicate his life. Friends who know Dr. Smith more intimately than I do say that he spends the first part of each day in prayer.

All who know my writings, and especially the prefaces written to various books through the years, are aware that I am not one given to carelessly uttered eulogies, but <u>my amazement at what Dr. Smith has accomplished compels me to write as I have done in this preface.</u>

This is the author's third book on prophecy. It is clear, biblical, inspiring, and most appropriate for an hour such as this. When a servant of God has

INTRODUCTION

been a lifelong student of the Holy Scriptures, has, for over forty years, engaged in a ministry which has been constantly attended by the presence and power of the Holy Spirit, has been the instrument through whom God has brought many into a living relationship with Christ, and has sent many out to the four corners of the earth to preach the Gospel, I am not only willing, but compelled at least to listen to what such a man has to say about the prophetic Scriptures. This is doubly true when, as with Dr. Smith, he is riding no hobbies, is presenting no fantastic theories, and is setting no dates.

This volume has two primary and most commendable characteristics: First of all, it centres in the person of our Lord Jesus Christ, and, secondly, it is saturated with the Word of God. Just this week I have read three articles brought together in a well-known theological quarterly, in which three professors in divinity schools in our country, two of them being of international reputation, discuss "Christ, the Hope of the World." In not one of these articles is a single verse quoted from the New Testament in which the word "hope" appears; nor do any of the authors seem to know anything about, or at least look for, the return of Christ.

In all discussions on prophetic themes, the major business of any writer or teacher is to examine what the Word of God has to say. This is exactly what

INTRODUCTION

Dr. Smith has done in his discussion of the coming King. It is a pleasure and privilege to commend the book in a prefatory word. May the Lord use it to persuade many to follow the Bereans of old, who examined the Scriptures to see if these things be true.

TABLE OF CONTENTS

		Page
	INTRODUCTION	5

Chapter
1. WHEN THE KING COMES BACK TO REIGN ... 15
2. WHEN THE KINGDOM HAS BEEN ESTABLISHED ... 26
3. WHEN THE PROPHETS SAW THE KINGDOM ... 33
4. WHEN ISAIAH SAW THE KING ... 59
5. WHEN JEREMIAH SAW THE KINGDOM AGE ... 83
6. WHEN EZEKIEL SAW THE KING ... 91
7. WHEN DANIEL SAW THE KINGDOM ... 99
8. WHEN THE PSALMIST SAW THE KING ... 109
9. WHEN THE APOSTLES SAW THE KINGDOM ... 115

CHAPTER I

WHEN THE KING COMES BACK TO REIGN

IS JESUS CHRIST coming back to reign on this earth? Will there be a literal Millennium? Do the Scriptures predict a kingdom of God characterized by righteousness and peace? Is the throne of David as real as the throne of Britain? Or are we to spiritualize the words of the prophet? Will the King come back to reign?

Throughout the Old Testament Scriptures we are told of a world-wide dispersion. The Jews were to become wanderers among the nations. Were these predictions fulfilled? Did the dispersion take place? Was Israel carried away captive? Does history record such a dispersion? Are we to take these prophecies literally, or should they be spiritualized?

<u>I know very few of the old commentaries that are trustworthy when it comes to prophecy.</u> Nearly all of them spiritualize the predictions of the Old Testament prophets and confuse the kingdom with the Church. Hence, their interpretations are worthless.

WHEN THE KING COMES BACK

There *was* a world-wide dispersion. Israel *was* carried away captive. These dispersions were literal. For more than two thousand years now the Jews have been wanderers among the nations.

What, then, about a national restoration? Will it, too, be literal? Or are we to spiritualize all the predictions of a reigning Messiah? Are we to understand that the prophecies concerning the kingdom are all fulfilled in the Church? I do not think so. In fact, I am sure about it. If the predictions regarding the dispersion are to be interpreted literally, then we have no alternative but to interpret the predictions that have to do with the restoration in the same way. They have nothing whatever to do with the Church, regardless of what the great commentators have to say. Such interpretations are most misleading.

"The prophets . . . testified beforehand the sufferings of Christ, and the glory that should follow" (1 Pet. 1: 10, 11; 4: 13; 5: 1; Luke 24: 26). Do we take the predictions regarding the sufferings of Christ literally? Of course we do. Then why not the predictions of His glory? They, too, will be fulfilled, every one of them; otherwise the prophets spoke falsely and the Old Testament is not God's book. How dare we spiritualize His glory when we do not spiritualize His sufferings? What right have we to say it is all fulfilled in the Church when we

WHEN THE KING COMES BACK TO REIGN

know perfectly well that a kingdom has been promised, a kingdom to be set up on earth? No, my friends, every prediction will be literally fulfilled.

ISAIAH'S GREAT PREDICTION

Look if you will at Isaiah's amazing prediction. You will find it in Isaiah 9: 6, 7:

"For unto us a child is born, unto us a son is given: and the government shall be upon his shoulder: and his name shall be called Wonderful, Counsellor, The mighty God, The everlasting Father, The Prince of Peace. Of the increase of his government and peace there shall be no end, upon the throne of David, and upon his kingdom, to order it, and to establish it with judgment and with justice from henceforth even for ever."

This passage says that the government shall be upon His shoulder. That prediction has never yet been fulfilled, nor will it be fulfilled until Jesus Christ returns and establishes His kingdom upon the earth. Then all nations will be governed by Him.

Furthermore, Isaiah makes it clear that His government will be characterized by peace. Hence, for the first time in the history of the world, war will be no more, for there will be peace among the nations. That prediction has never yet been fulfilled nor will it be until He reigns.

WHEN THE KING COMES BACK

Then, too, Isaiah mentions the throne of David. Jesus Christ is the legal successor to David's throne. He will be the next King of Israel. He is to sit on the throne of His father David and reign in millennial splendour and power for a thousand years.

Last of all, His reign is to be characterized by judgment and justice. For the first time in the history of the world, justice will be meted out amongst all nations.

THE ANGEL'S ANNOUNCEMENT TO MARY

Turn now to Luke 1: 31–33, where the Angel Gabriel visits the Virgin Mary. This is what he says:

"And, behold, thou shalt conceive in thy womb, and bring forth a son, and shalt call his name JESUS. He shall be great, and shall be called the Son of the Highest: and the Lord God shall give unto him the throne of his father David: And he shall reign over the house of Jacob forever; and of his kingdom there shall be no end."

Much in these verses has been fulfilled, but not all. In the angel's message we have that wonderful statement about the Lord Jesus Christ, namely that the Lord God shall give unto Him the throne of His father David. It is clear, then, that the throne of David is to be established once more and that Jesus Christ is to succeed David as King.

WHEN THE KING COMES BACK TO REIGN

Moreover, we are told that He is to reign over the house of Jacob; that He is to have a kingdom. All this, of course, is future. At His first advent He was not given the throne of His father David. He did not reign over the house of Jacob, nor was His kingdom established. What right have we to interpret verse 31 literally, then spiritualize verses 32 and 33?

THE ANSWER TO THE WISE MEN

In Matthew 2: 6 we have these words:

"And thou Bethlehem, in the land of Juda, art not the least among the princes of Juda: for out of thee shall come a Governor, that shall rule my people Israel."

Jesus Christ most certainly was born in Bethlehem, but at the time of His first advent He did not become a Governor, nor did He rule the people of Israel. All that is still future. It cannot be spiritualized. When He comes again in His glory, He will then rule over Israel as their Governor.

CHRIST'S FIRST MESSAGE

We must now look at Matthew 4: 17:

"From that time Jesus began to preach, and to say, Repent: for the kingdom of heaven is at hand."

WHEN THE KING COMES BACK

Also Matthew 19: 28:

"And Jesus said unto them, Verily I say unto you, That ye which have followed me, in the regeneration when the Son of man shall sit in the throne of his glory, ye also shall sit upon twelve thrones, judging the twelve tribes of Israel."

In these passages first of all the kingdom is announced. It is at hand. We know, of course, that it was rejected. Then Jesus speaks of a time called "the regeneration," or making over anew, the time when He sits on the throne of His glory, namely, David's throne. And He says that at that time His twelve apostles will sit with Him on twelve thrones and that they will judge the twelve tribes of Israel.

All this, of course, has never yet taken place. It is still future. It will be literally fulfilled when the King comes back to reign, and it will be during the period called the Millennium, or, as stated here, *the regeneration.*

PILATE'S QUESTION AND ACCUSATION

In Matthew 27: 11, 37, we have one or two very striking statements. The first is a question and it is asked by Pilate. "Art thou the King of the Jews?" he enquires. "Thou sayest," was the answer given by Jesus. Then there is the superscription that was

WHEN THE KING COMES BACK TO REIGN

placed on the cross. Matthew quotes it as follows: "THIS IS JESUS THE KING OF THE JEWS."

All this makes it very clear that Jesus was recognized as a King, and yet He was anything but a King at the time of His death. How then, are we to understand it? Unless He returns it cannot be understood. To spiritualize it is impossible. He was born a King. He died a King. He is coming again as a King. When He returns He will be a King in every sense of the word. And, of course, a king must have a kingdom. <u>His kingdom is to be right here on earth</u>. Hence there will be a kingdom and Jesus Christ will reign as King.

THE PLEA OF THE THIEF

In Luke 23: 42 the dying thief, you will remember, cried out, "Lord, remember me when thou comest into thy kingdom." In some marvellous way it was revealed to the penitent thief that the One who was hanging beside him on the centre cross was a King and that He had a kingdom. In his dying moments he was given faith to believe that that kingdom would one day be established and that the One who was dying by his side would reign as King. Hence his request. He wanted to be remembered in the day when the kingdom would be established by the One who was to be King.

WHEN THE KING COMES BACK

And, of course, he will be remembered. There is no doubt about that. When Jesus Christ returns in glory to establish His millennial kingdom upon earth, the dying thief, who met Him that very day in Paradise, will be remembered and will share in His reign, as will all others who are faithful to Him now.

THE ASCENSION QUESTION

Jesus had dealt with scores of prophetic events, but there was one point that He had not touched. Hence in Acts 1: 6, 7 we have a question asked by His disciples and immediately answered. Just as He was about to ascend into Heaven they asked, "Lord, wilt thou at this time restore again the kingdom to Israel? And he said unto them, It is not for you to know the times or the seasons, which the Father hath put in his own power."

This passage is of paramount importance. The disciples recognized that Israel did have a kingdom in centuries past and gone. They were referring, of course, to the kingdom under David and Solomon. Full well they knew that that kingdom had ceased to exist, but at the same time, they were well aware of the scores upon scores of predictions in the Old Testament Scriptures regarding the restoration of that kingdom. Hence their question.

Now Jesus did not rebuke them. He did not tell

WHEN THE KING COMES BACK TO REIGN

them that they had misunderstood the prophets, and that all the predictions about the kingdom were to be spiritualized and applied to the Church. That was left for the commentators. If His disciples had misunderstood the predictions, He most certainly would have said so; but, He knew their interpretation was correct and that there would be a kingdom. Hence all He said was that it was not for them to know the time when the kingdom would be set up. What else could He say? There was to be a kingdom and He was to be the King. That He knew. When He comes again the kingdom will be restored.

THE PRAYER OF THE CHURCH

We close our study with Matthew 6: 10:

"Thy kingdom come. Thy will be done in earth, as it is in heaven."

Do we still offer that prayer? If we do, then the kingdom has not yet come. If the prophecies are to be interpreted spiritually, and if the kingdom has already come, then we have no right to continue offering the prayer, "Thy kingdom come." If it has come, it is here; the prayer has been answered. But you and I know perfectly well that the kingdom has not yet been established and that Jesus Christ is not yet reigning on the throne of His father David.

WHEN THE KING COMES BACK

How do we know that this prayer has never yet been answered? Because it says very definitely that when the kingdom comes God's will will be done on earth exactly as it is now done in Heaven. Is there anyone in the world who would have the audacity to say that the will of God is now being done on earth as it is being done in Heaven? I think not. The Devil's will is being done today on earth. He is the god of this age. It will not be until Jesus Christ returns in millennial power and glory to reign on David's throne, that the will of God will be done on earth as it is being done in Heaven. When that day dawns, then, and not until then, the kingdom will have come. The prayer of the Church will be answered, and never again will it be necessary to offer the petition, "Thy kingdom come."

These prophecies, I maintain, must be literally fulfilled. If not, then the predictions of the Old Testament prophets are absolutely meaningless. They cannot, as the old commentators insist, be interpreted spiritually. The kingdom is not the Church. The Old Testament prophets did not even see the Church Age. They prophesied of God's dealings with Israel. Hence they spoke both of a suffering and a glorified Messiah. When He came the first time, He suffered. When He comes the second time, He will be glorified. When He came the first time, He was despised and put to death.

WHEN THE KING COMES BACK TO REIGN

When he comes the second time, He will reign in majestic splendour. When He came the first time, He came as a babe. When He comes the second time, He will come as a King. The promise of peace upon earth and goodwill among men has yet to be fulfilled.

If we accept the predictions regarding His first advent literally, then why not those that refer to His second? His sufferings were literal. Why should not His glory be literal also? The dispersion was a literal fact. It actually took place. Why not the restoration? Do the Scriptures, then, predict a kingdom on this earth, with Jesus Christ reigning as King? They most certainly do. All will be fulfilled when the King comes back to reign.

Millennium

CHAPTER 2

WHEN THE KINGDOM HAS BEEN ESTABLISHED

ALL THROUGH THE Bible the kingdom is clearly protrayed. It was promised to David and his seed. The prophets proclaimed it. Over nineteen hundred years ago the King was born. As soon as He commenced His ministry, He announced that the kingdom was "at hand". But the Jews rejected it. "We will not have this man to reign over us," they declared. They then arrested the King and crucified Him.

But according to the Scriptures, the King who is now absent is to return in glory, destroy His enemies and usher in the kingdom. But He must do it. The Church cannot. <u>There can be no kingdom without a king, and so the King Himself must come, or there will never be a kingdom.</u> He is David's greater Son, the legal successor to the Davidic throne; and when He comes again He will come, not as a babe, but as a King.

When the King comes back to reign, the kingdom will be established, first of all, over restored

WHEN THE KINGDOM IS ESTABLISHED

Israel; not only Judah, but all twelve tribes. As God showed Ezekiel, the two sticks will become one. Israel is to be regathered and converted. Then the kingdom will become world-wide.

ISRAEL RESTORED

So then, Israel will be restored to the land of Palestine, not in unbelief but in faith. Their hearts will be turned to God and once again they will serve Him. The Spirit will be poured out upon them, and looking on Him whom they have pierced, they will accept Him as their Messiah.

Moreover, they will be settled in Palestine and Jerusalem will become the capital city in the Golden Age, with Jesus Christ reigning on the throne of His father, David. In other words, <u>His government will be centralized in Zion</u>. All this the prophets clearly foretell. To spiritualize it is to cast doubt on the Word of God.

His kingdom will be established with violence and in the midst of judgment and catastrophe. The Church does not bring it in. The world does not get better and better. "Wicked men . . . wax worse and worse," the Bible says. Then Jesus comes and smites the nations, overthrowing them suddenly, after which His kingdom fills the whole earth. It is Daniel's smiting stone. Such is the teaching of Scripture.

WHEN THE KING COMES BACK

RIGHTEOUSNESS AND PEACE

The kingdom will be characterized by righteousness and peace, and war will be no more. For the first time in six thousand years there will be peace, justice and righteousness. Bloodshed will be a thing of the past, for the nations will never fight again. Battleships, ammunition, guns, bayonets, and bombs will be abolished. There will be no more taxes for defence. Violence, brutality and cruelty will be gone and gone for ever.

Moreover, long life will be restored, for there will be but little sickness. Deadly germs will be annihilated and all will be healthy, well and strong. If a man dies at the age of a hundred, his death will be looked upon as the death of a child. Like the patriarchs of old men will again live to be hundreds of years of age.

Every outbreak of sin will be instantly punished. No wrongdoing will be tolerated. The wicked will be in the minority, so much so, that the knowledge of the Lord will cover the earth as the waters fill the seas. Most of earth's inhabitants will be saved.

Even the nature of the wild beasts of the forest will be changed. Meat-eating animals will eat straw like the ox. No longer will they prey on one another. Lions, leopards, calves and wolves will live together

WHEN THE KINGDOM IS ESTABLISHED

in peace and harmony, eating the same grain and never again molesting one another. Little children will be safe in the woods where once the wild beasts roamed.

ABUNDANCE OF EVERYTHING

Then, too, <u>the earth will produce abundantly</u>, for the desert will bloom and blossom like the rose. The whole world will become a Garden of Eden, for the curse will be lifted and the ground will yield a rich and bountiful harvest. There will be plenty for everyone, fruit, grain and vegetables in abundance. No one will lack, no one go hungry. The multiplied millions of earth will be more than satisfied. Never again will there be a famine; all will have enough.

Most important of all, <u>Satan will be removed from the scene</u>. At long last, man's arch enemy will be imprisoned. Hence, he will deceive the nations no more. That, to a large extent, will account for the absence of sin and lawlessness. Temptation will be gone, for the tempter will be chained.

The <u>Kingdom Age will last for a thousand years</u>, a full Sabbath Day. Many think six days of a thousand years each will have gone; then will come the seventh, and for a thousand years Jesus Christ will reign at Jerusalem in millennial splendour, power and glory, as Lord of lords and King of kings.

WHEN THE KING COMES BACK

Oh, what spiritual, physical and intellectual heights men will then experience!

NO KINGDOM WITHOUT A KING

All this, and much more, is most vividly portrayed by the prophets. They did not see the Church; therefore, they did not speak or write of the Church. But they saw the kingdom; they saw the restoration, the regathering and conversion of Israel. They saw the coming of the King and the establishment and prosperity of the kingdom. They saw the overthrow of all Gentile nations and the glories of the kingdom.

I say, they saw the coming of the King, for there can be no kingdom without a King, and not until the Prince of Peace is here will this old war-torn world of ours know peace. It is all connected with the personal return of the Lord Jesus Himself. He has gone, but He is coming back. His feet will again tread the dirt roads of earth.

Jerusalem will then become the richest and the most glorious of all cities, for it will be the City of the great King. No wonder Isaiah broke forth in words of rapture when he cried, "And the Redeemer shall come to Zion," and again, "Arise, shine; for thy light is come, and the glory of the Lord is risen upon thee." Thus will it be when the kingdom has been established.

WHEN THE KINGDOM IS ESTABLISHED

Though the darkness and gloom triumphant
    O'er the whole of the world abides,
And the armies of Evil conquer
    Till there seemeth no pow'r besides;
Though the sword with its wake of sorrow,
    And the fields where the battles rage,
Seem to mock at the Prince of Salem,
    And the Hope of the Coming Age—

Yet the kingdom is surely coming,
    By the prophets so long foretold,
When the sword shall be sheathed forever
    In a peace that can ne'er grow old;
For the King will Himself, 'tis promised,
    In millennial splendour reign,
And the world overflow with gladness,
    For His plan shall at last be plain.

Though the kingdoms of earth in council
    On the wisdom of man rely,
And refuse to accept the offer
    Of the Lord who is ever nigh;
Though the forces of Wrong be many,
    And the armies of Right but few,
Though the works of the godless triumph,
    And the False overthrow the True—

Yet the kingdom is surely coming,
    By the prophets so long foretold,
When the sword shall be sheathed forever
    In a peace that can ne'er grow old;
For the King will Himself, 'tis promised,
    In millennial splendour reign,
And the world overflow with gladness,
    For His plan shall at last be plain.

Though the Hope of the Ages tarry
    Ere the prayers of the Church prevail,
And the darkness of sin and evil
    All the forces of Light assail;

WHEN THE KING COMES BACK

Though the sorrows of persecution,
    For the sake of the Saviour's cause,
Overshadow the brighter vision
    And the promise of righteous laws—

Yet the kingdom is surely coming,
    By the prophets so long foretold,
When the sword shall be sheathed forever
    In a peace that can ne'er grow old;
For the King will Himself, 'tis promised,
    In millennial splendour reign,
And the world overflow with gladness,
    For His plan shall at last be plain.

—O.J.S.

Millennium ✓

CHAPTER 3

WHEN THE PROPHETS SAW THE KINGDOM

IN 2 PETER 1: 19–21, we find these words:

"We have also a more sure word of prophecy; whereunto ye do well that ye take heed, as unto a light that shineth in a dark place, until the day dawn, and the day star arise in your hearts: Knowing this first, that no prophecy of the scripture is of any private interpretation. For the prophecy came not in old time by the will of man: but holy men of God spake as they were moved by the Holy Ghost."

Now let us see just what it was that these men, "moved by the Holy Ghost," saw and wrote concerning the kingdom. And let us note how completely they agreed with one another, even when they lived and wrote hundreds of years apart, proving conclusively that their revelation came from God. Nor are we going to dishonour God by spiritualizing their utterances. We will take them as they read.

WHEN THE KING COMES BACK

HOSEA

Turn first to Hosea 1: 10, 11:

"Yet the number of the children of Israel shall be as the sand of the sea, which cannot be measured nor numbered; and it shall come to pass, that in the place where it was said unto them, Ye are not my people, there it shall be said unto them, Ye are the sons of the living God. Then shall the children of Judah and the children of Israel be gathered together, and appoint themselves one head, and they shall come up out of the land."

God's people, Israel, are indestructible. Other nations have been destroyed, but not the Jews. In spite of all attempts to exterminate them, they are yet to become so numerous as to be compared to the sand of the sea. What a prospect!

Then, too, they are to be converted and to be recognized as "the sons of the living God". I am so glad that God lives and that because He lives they shall live also, for unlike the gods of the heathen, He is the living God.

Moreover, Israel and Judah are to be united. The Northern and the Southern kingdoms will once again be one. The remnants of the lost ten tribes will then be found.

Finally, they will acknowledge one head, one leader, one king, and that Head will be their one

WHEN THE PROPHETS SAW THE KINGDOM

time rejected Messiah, the Lord Jesus Christ, as we will see from other predictions.

Now Hosea 2:18-23:

"And in that day will I make a covenant for them with the beasts of the field, and with the fowls of heaven, and with the creeping things of the ground: and I will break the bow and the sword and the battle out of the earth, and will make them to lie down safely. And I will betroth thee unto me for ever; yea, I will betroth thee unto me in righteousness, and in judgment, and in loving kindness, and in mercies. I will even betroth thee unto me <u>in faithfulness</u>: and <u>thou shalt know the Lord</u>.

"And it shall come to pass in that day, I will hear, saith the Lord, I will hear the heavens, and they shall hear the earth; And the earth shall hear the corn, and the wine and the oil; and they shall hear Jezreel. And I will sow her unto me in the earth; and I will have mercy upon her that had not obtained mercy; and I will say to them which were not my people, Thou art my people; and they shall say, Thou art my God."

"That day" refers to the day of the Lord, the day that ushers in the Kingdom Age.

War will be no more. "I will break the bow and the sword and the battle," God says. Something will happen to the wild beasts, for it will be safe to lie down anywhere.

All Israel will know the Lord, for in mercy and

WHEN THE KING COMES BACK

loving kindness God will woo them to Himself. They shall be His people and He will be their God.

Next, Hosea 3: 4, 5:

"For the children of Israel shall abide many days without a king, and without a prince, and without a sacrifice, and without an image, and without an ephod, and without teraphim: Afterward shall the children of Israel return, and seek the Lord their God, and David their king; and shall fear the Lord and his goodness in the latter days."

For centuries they have been without a king or sacrifice; they were forsaken of God. But they will turn to Him again. It will be "in the latter days", when Jesus Christ comes back. Again and again He is called David, for He is David's greater Son. He will then become their King. At long last they will seek and fear the Lord, for all Israel shall be saved.

A world-wide dispersion is predicted in Hosea 9: 17, "My God will cast them away, because they did not hearken unto him: and they shall be wanderers among the nations." Was it literally fulfilled? It most certainly was. These other passages predict a national restoration and conversion. Will they, too, be fulfilled? I believe they will. We have no right to spiritualize either.

WHEN THE PROPHETS SAW THE KINGDOM

JOEL

Our text here is Joel 2: 28–32:

"And it shall come to pass afterward, that I will pour out my spirit upon all flesh; and your sons and your daughters shall prophesy, your old men shall dream dreams, your young men shall see visions: And also upon the servants and upon the handmaids in those days will I pour out my spirit. And I will shew wonders in the heavens and in the earth, blood, and fire, and pillars of smoke. The sun shall be turned into darkness, and the moon into blood, before the great and the terrible day of the Lord come. And it shall come to pass, that whosoever shall call on the name of the Lord shall be delivered: for in mount Zion and in Jerusalem shall be deliverance, as the Lord hath said, and in the remnant whom the Lord shall call."

There was an outpouring of the Spirit on the day of Pentecost, but "afterward" refers to "the last days" and the greater outpouring is still future.

For in that day there will be the signs mentioned by Jesus and here predicted by Joel, "blood, and fire, and pillars of smoke", the sun in darkness—a terrible day, until at last from Jerusalem comes deliverance, for, as stated in Joel 3: 17 and 21, "the Lord dwelleth in Zion." Says Jesus, "I am the Lord your God dwelling in Zion." So then Jesus

WHEN THE KING COMES BACK

Christ is to take up His abode in the city of Jerusalem and deliver His people. He is called both "Lord" and "God", and since it is Jesus Himself who returns and reigns, then Jesus is God. Thus Joel confirms His deity.

Jesus is God. He resides in Jerusalem. The city will at last be holy. No strangers to God will walk its streets.

There will be a superabundance of everything needed—wine, milk, water, etc. Only those who have been in Jerusalem know the dirth of water, but in that day it will be plentiful. Generation after generation will know no change. "Judah shall dwell forever." Wonderful age!

AMOS

Let us look at Amos 9: 11—15:

"In that day will I raise up the tabernacle of David that is fallen, and close up the breaches thereof; and I will raise up his ruins, and I will build it as in the days of old: That they may possess the remnant of Edom, and of all the heathen, which are called by my name, saith the Lord that doeth this.

"Behold, the days come, saith the Lord, that the ploughman shall overtake the reaper, and the treader of grapes him that soweth seed; and the mountains shall drop sweet wine, and all the hills shall melt.

WHEN THE PROPHETS SAW THE KINGDOM

"And I will bring again the captivity of my people of Israel, and they shall build the waste cities, and inhabit them; and they shall plant vineyards, and drink the wine thereof; they shall also make gardens, and eat the fruit of them.

"And I will plant them upon their land, and they shall no more be pulled up out of their land which I have given them, saith the Lord thy God."

This is one of the most important prophetic statements in all Scripture. It is quoted in Acts 15: 16, 17. The tabernacle or throne of David which has fallen is to be restored as in the days of old.

"That day" again refers to the day of the Lord, the end of the age, the ushering in of the next. It is still future.

Again we are told that there will be a superabundance of everything. The harvester will not be able to garner in the harvest before it will be time to plant another, so plentiful will it be.

All Israel will be regathered and restored to the land of Palestine, where they will rebuild, plant and sow and then reap the labours of their hands. Palestine will produce abundantly. No waste places will be left anywhere. The entire country will bloom and blossom as the rose.

Never again will there be a dispersion. Never again will they be driven out. Never again will their possessions be taken away from them. Foreign nations will molest them no more. Such is to be the future of Israel during the Kingdom Age.

MICAH

We read here from Micah 4: 1–8:

"*But in the last days it shall come to pass, that the mountain of the house of the Lord shall be established in the top of the mountains, and it shall be exalted above the hills; and people shall flow unto it.*

"*And many nations shall come, and say, Come, and let us go up to the mountain of the Lord, and to the house of the God of Jacob; and he will teach us his ways, and we will walk in his paths: for the law shall go forth of Zion, and the word of the Lord from Jerusalem.*

"*And he shall judge among many people, and rebuke strong nations afar off; and they shall beat their swords into ploughshares, and their spears into pruninghooks: nation shall not lift up a sword against nation, neither shall they learn war any more.*

"*But they shall sit every man under his vine and under his fig tree; and none shall make them afraid: for the mouth of the Lord of hosts hath spoken it. For all people will walk every one in the name of his god, and we will walk in the name of the Lord our God for ever and ever.*

"*In that day, saith the Lord, will I assemble her*

WHEN THE PROPHETS SAW THE KINGDOM

that halteth, and I will gather her that is driven out, and her that I have afflicted; And I will make her that halted a remnant, and her that was cast far off a strong nation: and the Lord shall reign over them in mount Zion from henceforth, even for ever.

"And thou, O tower of the flock, the strong hold of the daughter of Zion, unto thee shall it come, even the first dominion; the kingdom shall come to the daughter of Jerusalem."

This is, without exception, one of the most wonderful descriptions ever penned of the Golden Age. How the old commentators could spiritualize it, I can't for the life of me understand. It will all come to pass. It is not the Church, it is the kingdom, and it will be literally fulfilled just as the numerous predictions regarding the captivity in Babylon were literally fulfilled.

It is to take place in "the last days". We have not yet seen those days. Hence, it has nothing whatever to do with the first advent. It will not be fulfilled until He comes again.

The kingdom, we are told, will be above all others. The so-called great powers, as well as the weaker nations, will all be subject to it. As Daniel says, it will fill the whole earth. Hence, it will be supreme.

Moreover, it will be a universal kingdom. "Many nations, many people," God says. All nations will be subject to it.

WHEN THE KING COMES BACK

Most of the people of the world will then be converted. They will walk in the ways of the Lord and listen to His teaching. From the capital, the city of Jerusalem, He will instruct the people of all nations.

NO MORE WAR

It will be an age of peace. At long last war will end. Never again will sons, husbands and brothers be sent away to fight and die. "They shall beat their swords into ploughshares, and their spears into pruninghooks; nation shall not lift up sword against nation, neither shall they learn war any more (Isa. 2: 4). Oh, what a day!

If there is one thing we hate more than another, it is war. In Genesis 6: 11 it says that "the earth was filled with violence". Now God hates violence. That was one reason He sent the flood. Violence, brutality, cruelty and bloodshed, are all to be eliminated in the Kingdom Age (Isa. 60: 18). In that day war will be outlawed. One government and one King will keep the peace. Aggression will be no more. No longer will our battle fleets sail the seas. Cannons, guns, bayonets, armaments, and atomic bombs will all be scrapped. Men will kill no more.

WHEN THE PROPHETS SAW THE KINGDOM

THE RIGHTS OF MAN

"They shall sit every man under his vine and under his fig tree." Private enterprise and private ownership will be the order of the New Age. If it has been lost, it will be restored. The dignity of the individual will be recognized once more. Each man will have his own possessions. Nor will there be any fear of State ownership or collective farming. Socialism and communism are unknown in the Bible. "Thou shalt not covet" is still God's Word. No longer will the individual be robbed by his government by means of taxation. What he has acquired by his skill and labour will never be taken from him. No one will trespass on another's property. Sitdown strikes on the premises of others will never be tolerated. Fear of government confiscation will be gone forever. Man will be able to accumulate and save without the dread of having it taken from him. Thriftiness and honest toil will at last be rewarded.

Oppressive taxes have always been an abomination, and from time immemorial tax collectors have been despised. As a matter of fact, the Word of God has mentioned certain individuals as exempt altogether from taxtaion. Turn, if you will, to Ezra 7: 24, and you will find that even a pagan government considered those responsible for the Lord's work free from taxes. The verse reads as follows:

"Also we certify you, that touching any of the priests and Levites, singers, porters, Nethinims, or ministers of this house of God, *it shall not be lawful* to impose toll, tribute, or custom, upon them."

Men should be encouraged by every possible means to spend their money for the erection of large and beautiful homes, with lovely well-kept gardens to adorn the landscape and make the world more beautiful to the eye. The building and care of these homes and gardens could provide work for countless thousands in a congenial atmosphere and amid pleasant surroundings.

Today, if a man adds to the value of his property, he pays additional taxes. That is a vicious system. Every dollar spent is an asset to the community. As an inducement to do more, taxes should be lowered, otherwise we will hoard when we should spend. Our beautiful homes and gardens are rapidly disappearing because of a shortsighted system of taxation; whereas they should be multiplying by tens of thousands.

To take money from those who have saved and invested, those who have never squandered, those who neither drink nor smoke, but have been industrious and thrifty, then to give it to spendthrifts and n'er-do-wells who have wasted their substance in riotous living and have made no effort to save, those who do not want to work, is unjust and un-christian.

WHEN THE PROPHETS SAW THE KINGDOM

Aside from essential tribute for government support no government has the right to take from man that which he has earned, whether it is taken by brute force as in totalitarian states or by man-made laws as in other countries; it is nothing short of highway robbery. The socialist demand to legally "distribute the wealth" is wrong. Legal procedure does not change God's fundamental law against theft. The Bible says, "Thou shalt not steal", thus setting God's seal of approval on private ownership.

Man has the inalienable right to do what he will with his own. Therefore, in that day, death duties, gift and inheritance taxes, will be abolished. Today there are states that would rob him of the joy of Christian philanthropy and private investment. In the Bible parents are commanded to lay up for their children. How can they if the State takes it from them?

FREEDOM FOR ALL MANKIND

Freedom should be granted to all, freedom of religion, freedom of speech and freedom of assembly. By freedom of religion I mean freedom to propagate one's faith in any way and in any place he sees fit. It should be possible, even now, to hold meetings without government permission. Men should be permitted to say and newspapers to publish what they like, so long as the law against slander is recognized and the overthrow of the government by violence never advocated.

In some countries today you cannot choose your employer and you cannot quit your job, nor can you change it. You do what you are told to do all your life. Everyone is in complete and absolute dependence on the State. Anyone who opposes those in authority menaces his very existence. There are governments today under which you dare not drive a nail. Your home can never be yours; it is the property of the State. All that will be changed in the Millennial Age.

There was a time when they had real social security in America. The slaves had no worries. Their food was provided, their clothing and houses. Even medical attention cost them nothing. And their old age was assured. They had everything they needed, but—they were slaves. Strange, is it not, that white people should vote to becomes slaves. Yet that is exactly what is happening today. I think the Bible makes it clear that the best work will be done if the people are left as free as possible to shape their own destiny. Certain controls are necessary, but I deny with tens of thousands of others the right of the State to do everything for everyone, leaving the people with no more choice, initiative or freedom, than domestic animals. The individual is bound to do more for himself, his family

WHEN THE PROPHETS SAW THE KINGDOM

and his community, if allowed reasonable freedom to function and launch out. The State should keep the ring, see that the rules are observed, and protect the weak, but otherwise allow room for free play and healthy development. The less the government interferes, the happier the people will be.

Already we have gone too far. People have lost their morale. There was no government relief when I was a boy. Relatives and friends took care of the unfortunate until work could be found. The Bible says, "If any would not work, neither should he eat" (2 Thess. 3: 10). That is God's law—no work, no food. Our fathers created work if they could not find it. They had ambition. They were out to make good and they succeeded.

We know from the prophecies of God's Word that, as the age draws to a close, totalitarianism will triumph, for the iron will never mix with the clay. All governments must head up in the Antichrist, for he will be the sole ruler and dictator. Dictatorship will then be the order of the day.

Socialism, I say again, cannot be found in the Bible. In the early community of Christians, Christ was the centre. There is nothing like that in the socialism of today. The Bible from beginning to end endorses private enterprise and recognizes the dignity of the individual. See Matthew 20: 1–15. Both labour and management should study it.

WHEN THE KING COMES BACK

There is only One who knows how to govern this world and that One is the Lord Jesus Christ. Not until He returns and is accepted will we have peace, righteousness and justice for all. Only then will our problem be solved. As long as the world rejects its King, there will be chaos. God grant that the day may soon come when the kingdoms of this world will have become the kingdoms of our Lord and of his Christ.

ZEPHANIAH

Here we read Zephaniah 3: 9, 13–20:

"For then will I turn to the people a pure language, that they may all call upon the name of the Lord, to serve him with one consent.

"The remnant of Israel shall not do iniquity, nor speak lies; neither shall a deceitful tongue be found in their mouth: for they shall feed and lie down, and none shall make them afraid.

"Sing, O daughter of Zion; shout, O Israel; be glad and rejoice with all the heart, O daughter of Jerusalem. The Lord hath taken away thy judgments, he hath cast out thy enemy: the king of Israel, even the Lord, is in the midst of thee: thou shalt not see evil any more.

"In that day it shall be said to Jerusalem, Fear thou not: and to Zion, Let not thy hands be slack. The Lord thy God in the midst of thee is mighty; he will

WHEN THE PROPHETS SAW THE KINGDOM

save, he will rejoice over thee with joy; he will rest in his love, he will joy over thee with singing.

"I will gather them that are sorrowful for the solemn assembly, who are of thee, to whom the reproach of it was a burden. Behold, at that time I will undo all that afflicts thee: and I will save her that halteth, and gather her that was driven out; and I will get them praise and fame in every land where they have been put to shame.

"At that time will I bring you again, even in the time that I gather you: for I will make you a name and a praise among all people of the earth, when I turn back your captivity before your eyes, saith the Lord."

Here we have once again the conversion of the Gentiles and all of them calling upon and serving the Lord. Also the national conversion of Israel and their cleansing. No longer are they characterized by iniquity. At last they have become a holy nation. Hence, fear is gone; they can eat and sleep in peace. No one will ever threaten them again.

No wonder the prophet cries out, "Sing, O daughter of Zion; shout, O Israel; be glad and rejoice with all the heart, O daughter of Jerusalem. The Lord hath taken away thy judgments . . . thou shalt not see evil any more."

Now they can sing. What a change! For hundreds of years they have been in mourning for they have been out of their land and bitter persecution has

WHEN THE KING COMES BACK

been their lot. But at last they can be glad again. Once more they can rejoice. The great Smiting Stone has smitten the nations, their tribulations are ended and they will see evil no more.

The Lord Himself, their Messiah, will be in their midst, reigning at Jerusalem, strong to deliver and mighty to save. His joy over them will be as great as theirs over Him. Instead of being despised they will now be honoured and that by the very nations that at one time held them in shame and contempt. Their captivity will be ended and their chastisement forever past.

ZECHARIAH

First, Zechariah 2: 10:

"Sing and rejoice, O daughter of Zion: for, lo, I come, and I will dwell in the midst of thee, saith the Lord."

Well, here it is. At last He comes. Why should the people of Jerusalem sing and rejoice? Because their Messiah returns. And having come, He dwells with them in Zion. Oh, happy day! Christ is here again.

Second, Zechariah 3: 8:

"I will bring forth my servant the BRANCH."

Always, everywhere, the BRANCH is Jesus Christ.

Third, Zechariah 3: 10:

"In that day, saith the Lord of hosts, shall ye call every man his neighbour under the vine and under the fig tree."

WHEN THE PROPHETS SAW THE KINGDOM

Again it is "that day". Still future, of course. Here at last is security, a security, protection and safety never known before. But it cannot be until the King and the kingdom come.

Fourth, Zechariah 6: 12, 13:

"Behold the man whose name is The BRANCH; and he shall grow up out of his place, and he shall build the temple of the Lord: Even he shall build the temple of the Lord; and he shall bear the glory, and shall sit and <u>rule upon his throne; and he shall be a priest upon his throne</u>."

The BRANCH again—Jesus Christ. Not in His humility but in His glory, when He returns, for here He sits on a throne not only as a King but also as a Priest, for He is the Priest-King. At last He sits, not on His Father's throne, but on His own, the throne of His Father David.

Fifth, Zechariah 8: 3–8:

"Thus saith the Lord; I am returned unto Zion, and will dwell in the midst of Jerusalem: and Jerusalem shall be called a city of truth; and the mountain of the Lord of hosts the holy mountain.

"Thus saith the Lord of hosts; There shall yet old men and old women dwell in the streets of Jerusalem, and every man with his staff in his hand for very age. And the streets of the city shall be full of boys and girls playing in the streets thereof.

"And I will bring them, and they shall dwell in

WHEN THE KING COMES BACK

the midst of Jerusalem: and they shall be my people, and I will be their God, in truth and in righteousness."

Jesus says he has returned to Zion. He was there before, nearly two thousand years ago. He died there. Now He returns. Moreover, He takes up His residence there, and the kingdom is established in truth and holiness.

Long life will be restored. Deaths will be few. The aged will be honoured and there will be more of them living than ever before in the history of the world. No longer will men and women die young. Memories will be long. But along with the old will be the young—boys and girls. Little children, happy and carefree, will be seen playing in the streets. What a picture of joy and fullness of life!

So then, Jerusalem will be inhabited with a population never before equalled, all dwelling together as the people of God. Can you imagine such a city? Can you picture such a society? Earth has never yet seen it, but it will surely come to pass in God's tomorrow.

Sixth, Zechariah 8: 20–23:

"Thus saith the Lord of hosts; It shall yet come to pass, that there shall come people, and the inhabitants of many cities: And the inhabitants of one city shall go to another, saying, Let us go speedily to pray before the Lord.

"Thus saith the Lord of hosts; In those days it

WHEN THE PROPHETS SAW THE KINGDOM

shall come to pass, that ten men shall take hold out of all languages of the nations, even shall take hold of the skirt of him that is a Jew, saying, We will go with you: for we have heard that God is with you."

Now God Himself speaks and the words He speaks the prophet writes. "It shall yet come to pass." When God says that, He is writing history in advance and every word will be fulfilled.

It is a picture of a God-fearing world, people living in numerous cities, all anxious to please the Lord. The centre of worship will be the beloved city, Zion. The Jews are in high favour, so much so, that people of other nations vie with each other to worship with them. That has never happened, nor will it until Christ returns.

Seventh, Zechariah 9: 10:

"*And he shall speak peace unto the heathen: and his dominion shall be from sea even to sea, and from the river even to the ends of the earth.*"

What a promise! Never will the Gentile nations know peace in this world until Christ the Prince of Peace is enthroned. He and He alone is the One who speaks peace to the people.

"His dominion shall be from sea even to sea, and from the river even to the ends of the earth." That is one of the greatest utterances ever spoken about the rule, the reign, and the dominion of the Messiah. Most certainly it was not fulfilled at His

WHEN THE KING COMES BACK

first advent, except perhaps in a spiritual sense. It still awaits fulfilment. When He comes the second time He will come to reign and His kingdom in that day will be from sea to sea—world-wide, universal. What a Conqueror! Nebuchadnezzar, Alexander, Napoleon, all take second place. He will be greater than them all for He will rule the world. One government, one King, and one kingdom.

> Jesus shall reign where're the sun
> Does his successive journeys run;
> His kingdom spread from shore to shore,
> Till moons shall wax and wane no more.

Eighth, Zechariah 12: 10:

"And I will pour upon the house of David, and upon the inhabitants of Jerusalem, the spirit of grace and of supplications: and they shall look upon me whom they have pierced, and they shall mourn for him, as one mourneth for his only son, and shall be in bitterness for him, as one is in bitterness for his firstborn."

Hearts will be changed, changed by a mighty outpouring of the Spirit of God. Israel will be converted. The people of Jerusalem will at last be a godly people.

The next time they will see their Messiah will be after His return in glory. "They shall look upon me whom they have pierced." What an amazing

WHEN THE PROPHETS SAW THE KINGDOM

prediction! Crucifixion was a Roman invention. It was never Jewish. Yet here the prophet predicts the piercing of the Messiah. His hands and feet as well as His side were pierced. When they see Him again He will still bear the marks and they will immediately recognize Him, for they pierced Him. Pilate wanted His release; they demanded His death. The Romans would have let Him go; the Jews cried, "Away with him, crucify him."

At last they will admit that they crucified their Messiah and they will lament and mourn for Him in bitter, bitter anguish. When He came the first time, nearly two thousand years ago now, they pierced Him; when He comes the second time they will recognize Him, mourn over Him and accept Him.

Ninth, Zechariah 13: 1:

"In that day there shall be a fountain opened to the house of David and to the inhabitants of Jerusalem for sin and for uncleanness." Yes, in that day God will cleanse them from their sin and they shall be clean.

Tenth, Zechariah 14: 1–21. This is the greatest chapter in the book and one of the greatest in all prophecy. I am not going to quote it here. It should be read from the Word itself. I have devoted an entire chapter to an exposition of it in my book, *Prophecy—What Lies Ahead*.

WHEN THE KING COMES BACK

In verse 2 we have the Battle of Armageddon. Jerusalem is taken by the armies of the Antichrist, the houses robbed, the women ravished and half of the population taken captive. Then in their darkest hour, as related in verse three, the Lord Himself comes to their rescue.

When Jesus returns His feet will first touch the Mount of Olives. Not an imaginary mount, but the mount just outside Jerusalem. There will be an earthquake and the mount will move east and west, leaving a great valley running north and south.

The statement regarding His coming is most positive. "The Lord my God shall come and all the saints with thee." (See vs. 5.) Again Jesus is called God. He comes and with Him His raptured saints—the Church. This is His second coming. No saints came with Him when He came the first time.

Now comes the glorious announcement regarding His Kingship and His kingdom. "And the Lord shall be king over all the earth." Hallelujah! Jesus Christ will be King and His reign will be world-wide. It will be the first universal kingdom ever established. At His first advent, He was not a King. At His second, His Kingship is assured. "The Lord shall be king."

The mountains will be levelled. Great populations will inhabit the land. Jerusalem will at last, and for the first time, be a safe place of residence, and

WHEN THE PROPHETS SAW THE KINGDOM

will become, according to verse 14, the wealthiest city in the world. A great annual convocation will be held in the city, attended by representatives of all the nations, with instant and terrible judgment meted out to those who ignore it; and holiness will characterize the entire age.

MALACHI

Turn first to Malachi 3: 1–6. Beginning with His first coming and continuing with His second, we are informed in this passage that Christ will come suddenly and with judgment. He will so cleanse and purify His people that their service will be acceptable to Him. The wicked will be instantly punished, especially the spiritualist mediums and the immoral. Then, says God, "All nations will call you blessed: for ye shall be a delightsome land" (3: 12). What high honour! Israel will at last be exalted.

Then, Malachi 4: 1:

"For, behold, the day cometh, that shall burn as an oven; and all the proud, yea, and all that do wickedly, shall be stubble: and the day that cometh shall burn them up, saith the Lord of hosts, that it shall leave them neither root nor branch."

So the wicked will be gone.

WHEN THE KING COMES BACK

Last of all, Malachi 4: 2:

"But unto you that fear my name shall the Sun of righteousness arise with healing in his wings; and ye shall go forth, and grow up as calves of the stall. And ye shall tread down the wicked; for they shall be ashes under the soles of your feet in the day that I shall do this, saith the Lord of hosts."

Christ appears, the righteous flourish and the wicked are seen no more, for the millennium has come. Elijah will be His forerunner when He comes again, as John was the forerunner for His first advent (vss. 5, 6). The day of judgment must precede the day of glory. Thus have the prophets written and thus will it be.

CHAPTER 4

WHEN ISAIAH SAW THE KING

ISAIAH HAS MORE to say about the King and the kingdom than any other writer in the Bible. He saw both His sufferings and His glory, and he describes both. His sufferings we interpret literally. The fifty-third chapter, we all know, was fulfilled nearly two thousand years ago. If then, His sufferings are to be interpreted literally, why not His glory? What right have we to spiritualize the predictions concerning the kingdom and apply them to the Church? I believe they are to be interpreted literally. God meant what He said and said what He meant. He saw the end from the beginning. Let us hear, now, what Isaiah said when He saw the King.

NO MORE WAR

First of all, let us turn to Isaiah 2: 1–4:

"*The word that Isaiah the son of Amos saw concerning Judah and Jerusalem.*

"*And it shall come to pass in the last days, that the mountain of the Lord's house shall be established*

WHEN THE KING COMES BACK

in the top of the mountains, and shall be exalted above the hills; and all nations shall flow unto it.

"And many people shall go and say, Come ye, and let us go up to the mountain of the Lord, to the house of the God of Jacob; and he will teach us of his ways, and we will walk in his paths: for out of Zion shall go forth the law, and the word of the Lord from Jerusalem.

"And he shall judge among the nations, and shall rebuke many people: and they shall beat their swords into ploughshares, and their spears into pruning-hooks: nation shall not lift up sword against nation, neither shall they learn war any more."

God gave Micah this same vision (Micah 4: 1–8). It has to do with the tribe of Judah and the city of Jerusalem. God's kingdom is supreme over all. He controls all nations. Most people are God-fearing. Jerusalem is the centre of worship. War is forever outlawed. Jesus Christ is now the Ruler of the world. All this we have already seen in our study of Micah. Verses 11 and 17 tell us that man's day is over. At last he is humbled to the dust and the Lord alone is exalted. "The lofty looks of man shall be humbled, and the haughtiness of men shall be bowed down, and the Lord alone shall be exalted in that day."

With that majestic passage, Isaiah 9: 6, 7, we have already dealt. It proclaims Him King on

WHEN ISAIAH SAW THE KING

David's throne and tells us that Jesus Christ is God. What a prophecy!

PEACE AND RIGHTEOUSNESS

Let us read from Isaiah 11: 1-13; 12: 1-6:

"*And there shall come forth a rod out of the stem of Jesse, and a Branch shall grow out of his roots: And the spirit of the Lord shall rest upon him, the spirit of wisdom and understanding, the spirit of counsel and might, the spirit of knowledge and of the fear of the Lord; And shall make him of quick understanding in the fear of the Lord: and he shall not judge after the sight of his eyes, neither reprove after the hearing of his ears: But with righteousness shall he judge the poor, and reprove with equity for the meek of the earth: and he shall smite the earth with the rod of his mouth, and with the breath of his lips shall he slay the wicked. And righteousness shall be the girdle of his loins, and faithfulness the girdle of his veins.*

"*The wolf also shall dwell with the lamb, and the leopard shall lie down with the kid; and the calf and the young lion and the fatling together; and a little child shall lead them. And the cow and the bear shall feed; their young ones shall lie down together: and the lion shall eat straw like the ox. And the sucking child shall play on the hole of the asp, and the weaned child shall put his hand on the cockatrice's den. They shall not hurt nor destroy in all my holy mountain: for the earth shall be full of the knowledge of the Lord, as the waters cover the sea.*

"*And in that day there shall be a root of Jesse, which shall stand for an ensign of the people; to it shall the Gentiles seek: and his rest shall be glorious.*

"*And it shall come to pass in that day, that the Lord shall set his hand again the second time to recover the remnant of his people, which shall be left, from Assyria, and from Egypt, and from Pathros, and from Cush, and from Elam, and from Shinar, and from Hamath, and from the islands of the sea. And he shall set up an ensign for the nations, and shall assemble the outcasts of Israel, and gather together the dispersed of Judah from the four corners of the earth. The envy also of Ephraim shall depart, and the adversaries of Judah shall be cut off: Ephraim shall not envy Judah, and Judah shall not vex Ephraim.*"

"*And in that day thou shalt say, O Lord, I will praise thee: though thou wast angry with me, thine anger is turned away, and thou comfortedst me. Behold, God is my salvation; I will trust, and not be afraid; for the Lord JEHOVAH is my strength and my song; he also is become my salvation. Therefore with joy shall ye draw water out of the wells of salvation.*

"*And in that day shall ye say, Praise the Lord,*

WHEN ISAIAH SAW THE KING

call upon his name, declare his doings among the people, make mention that his name is exalted. Sing unto the Lord; for he hath done excellent things: this is known in all the earth. Cry out and shout, thou inhabitant of Zion: for great is the Holy One of Israel in the midst of thee."

SAFETY, BLESSING AND PROSPERITY

We have come now to one of the most glorious prophecies ever uttered. The entire passage has to do with the King and the kingdom. None of it was fulfilled at the first advent, and none of it can be spiritualized, for it has no fulfilment in the Church, in spite of what the great commentators say. God did not see fit to enlighten them. Knowledge was not to increase, according to Daniel, until the latter days.

The prophet begins by tracing the human ancestry of the King back to Jesse, the father of David. Once again Jesus is the Branch.

God's Spirit possesses Him, so that He is the wisest of the wise. He is the mighty Counsellor. All knowledge is His so that He does not err in judgment. He is always right. In Him the defenceless have a righteous Advocate. He speaks and it is done. The wicked are slain and the righteous exonerated.

WHEN THE KING COMES BACK

During His reign over the earth the instincts of animals are changed. No longer is it the law of the tooth and the fang. No longer must they kill or be killed. Even among the beasts of the earth, for the first time in history, there is friendship. Never before had the lamb dwelt with the wolf unless it was on the inside. Now both dwell together, while the leopard and the kid live in harmony. The calf and the lion become friends. And in the midst of it all, a little child—playfully and fearlessly—makes them his pets. Bears and cows feed side by side and their young sleep together in perfect safety, utterly unafraid. Even their appetite is changed, for the lion—a meat-eating animal—becomes domesticated and eats straw or hay as does the ox.

Then to prove that there is no danger anywhere, the prophet sees a little baby with its hand over the hole of the asp, and an older child at the den of a cockatrice, and he says, "They shall not hurt nor destroy in all my holy mountain". A mountain in prophecy is a kingdom. This mountain is God's kingdom. None will hurt, none will destroy in any part of that kingdom. There will be safety throughout the entire world during the reign of Christ. The Golden Age will at last become a reality, for the millennium will be here.

Can you picture such a world? Ferocious animals

become the pets of children. Blood ceases to flow, for they never kill again. Danger is an unknown word. Lions gambol on lawns. Wolves lose their fierceness. Leopards no longer lurk in their hiding places and spring on their victims. Little children know no danger, for safety is the order of the age.

I always have hated violence, brutality and cruelty, either to animals, to birds, or men. God does, too. In that day there will be no more destruction. Animals, birds and men will rise to their highest height of perfection and security and will at last fulfill their God-intended destiny. All will live together as a happy family, never again to hurt or destroy. What a picture! And what a day that will be!

WORLD-WIDE KNOWLEDGE OF GOD

Today the world knows but little of God. Most nations are almost entirely ignorant of Him. In that day, the prophet says, "the earth will be full of the knowledge of the Lord, as the waters cover the sea." How much of the sea is covered by water? All of it, is it not? So, too, will it be with the knowledge of God. All the world will know Him. The most backward island, the jungle of South America, the heart of Africa—all will be ablaze with the knowledge of the Lord. In that day there will be no more missionary work to be done. Now is the

WHEN THE KING COMES BACK

time to do it. If we do not do it now, we never will. In that day it will not be needed. The Lord will have made Himself known to all alive on the earth. The Eskimos in the Arctic, the savages in the great forests of Brazil, the Hottentots of Africa, the wild pygmies of the jungles—red, yellow, black and white—all will know Him in that day. <u>At last the world will be Christianized</u>, its people converted, and society, as a whole, become God-fearing and righteous. God speed the day; it cannot come too soon.

But who is the King, the Leader, the Ensign? "A root of Jesse." And who is that Root? Jesus Christ. Will it be for Israel alone? By no means. "To it shall the Gentiles seek." Thus the rule of Jesus Christ will be universal. All the nations of the world will submit to His authority. "His rest shall be glorious." Such glory mankind has never seen. The coronation of the Queen of England was glorious, but that glory will fade into insignificance in comparison to the glory of the King of kings. His kingdom, His rule, His reign, will be the most glorious ever known.

Israel will be regathered and restored. Once a few of them were brought back from Babylon, but now all of them will be brought from the nations of all the world, and restored to their own land. No longer will there by any jealousy, division, or

WHEN ISAIAH SAW THE KING

conflict among them. Ephraim and Judah will be reunited and will become one nation again. Oh, what a change! Once they fought each other. Now they are at peace.

A SPIRITUAL OUTPOURING

Moreover they will experience a great and wonderful outpouring of the Spirit, that will cause them to praise the Lord for His goodness to them. Their hearts will be changed and they will become a truly spiritual nation. At last they will be comforted. Their years of wandering over, they will find rest to their souls. Trust will take the place of fear. Praise will fill their hearts, and their songs will be of God and His mercy to them. "I will trust, and not be afraid," they will say. Oh, what joy will then be theirs! What exultation of spirit! Isaiah is beside himself as God reveals it to him, and he cries out, "Sing unto the Lord . . . Cry out and shout, thou inhabitant of Zion: for great is the Holy One of Israel in the midst of thee."

He sees the Messiah, Jesus Christ. He dwells in Jerusalem in the midst of His people Israel. Holy is He, holy and great, for He is God. And now, at long last, He is ruling over all the world. No wonder He is worshipped by His people, for is He not the Lord Jehovah Himself?

WHEN THE KING COMES BACK

Let all the world bow before Him, rulers and potentates, kings and queens—let them cast themselves at His feet and acclaim Him Lord of lords and King of kings. Take off your crown, ye kings; bare your heads, ye rulers; lay aside your badge of authority; bow the knee, ye people of the world, and worship at His throne.

> All hail the pow'r of Jesus' name!
> Let angels prostrate fall;
> Bring forth the royal diadem,
> And crown Him Lord of all!

In Isaiah 27: 6 we read, "Israel shall blossom and bud, and fill the face of the world with fruit." Yes, Israel will yet be a blessing. But it will not be until the Kingdom Age. Yet since there can be no kingdom without a king, in Isaiah 32: 1 the prophet predicts: "Behold, a king shall reign in righteousness." Did He reign at His first advent? He did not. Then when will He reign? When will Isaiah 32: 1 be fulfilled? When He comes again. Then He will reign, and righteousness will characterize His reign. For, with the outpouring of the Spirit, the nations will become righteous, and the earth fruitful. There will then be quietness, peace and assurance, as described in Isaiah 32: 15–18, "sure [or safe] dwellings, and in quiet resting places."

In Isaiah 33: 17 we read, "Thine eyes shall see

WHEN ISAIAH SAW THE KING

the king in his beauty: they shall behold the land that is very far off." Yes, in that day we shall see the King, the Lord Jesus Christ.

JERUSALEM IN THE GOLDEN AGE

Our passage here is Isaiah 33: 20–24:

"Look upon Zion, the city of our solemnities: thine eyes shall see Jerusalem a quiet habitation, a tabernacle that shall not be taken down; not one of the stakes thereof shall ever be removed, neither shall any of the cords thereof be broken. But there the glorious Lord will be unto us a place of broad rivers and streams; wherein shall go no galley with oars, neither shall gallant ship pass thereby. For the Lord is our judge, the Lord is our lawgiver, the Lord is our king; he will save us. And the inhabitant shall not say, I am sick: the people that dwell therein shall be forgiven their iniquity."

Now for a look at Jerusalem during the Golden Age. The city will be quiet. It never has been, but it will be. And then the glorious Lord will reign; He will reign as Judge, as Lawgiver, and as King.

The inhabitants of Jerusalem will be a forgiven people and a healthy people. Sickness will be no more. There will be no hospitals or clinics, and no asylums during the Kingdom Age. Doctors will

WHEN THE KING COMES BACK

have to seek another occupation, for none will be sick. The things that cause ill-health will be gone. The curse will be lifted, and germs will disappear. "How are you?" will not be the salutation, for all will be well. Homes for incurables will be put to other and better uses, for none shall say, "I am sick." Oh, what a life! Sick benefits will no longer be needed. God knows the cure for all diseases: leprosy, cancer, tuberculosis, diabetes, and a score of other afflictions that we have always thought of as incurable, will be remembered as belonging to the dark ages of the past. "The inhabitant shall not say, I am sick." Soul and body will both be well.

Sometimes, when I walk through wards and corridors of hospitals and see the pain-racked bodies on either side of me, or listen to their groans, my heart within me cries for that millennial day and age when there will be no more pain. Doctors and nurses may do what they can to relieve it now, but not until the Great Physician Himself takes over the government of the world will it be entirely eliminated. God never did intend that it should be. Pain in child-bearing is the result of sin. In that day "the people . . . shall be forgiven their iniquity." Hearts will be cleansed from sin; none will be sick; neither shall there be any more pain.

WHEN ISAIAH SAW THE KING

THE GLORIES OF THE MILLENNIUM

Turn now to Isaiah 35: 1–10:

"The wilderness and the solitary place shall be glad for them; and the desert shall rejoice, and blossom as the rose. It shall blossom abundantly, and rejoice even with joy and singing: the glory of Lebanon shall be given unto it, the excellency of Carmel and Sharon, they shall see the glory of the Lord, and the excellency of our God.

"Strengthen ye the weak hands, and confirm the feeble knees. Say to them that are of a fearful heart, Be strong, fear not: behold, your God will come with vengeance, even God with a recompense; he will come and save you.

"Then the eyes of the blind shall be opened, and the ears of the deaf shall be unstopped. Then shall the lame man leap as an hart, and the tongue of the dumb sing: for in the wilderness shall waters break out, and streams in the desert. And the parched ground shall become a pool, and the thirsty land springs of water: in the habitation of dragons, where each lay, shall be grass with reeds and rushes.

"And an highway shall be there, and a way, and it shall be called The way of holiness; the unclean shall not pass over it; but it shall be for those: the wayfaring men, though fools, shall not err therein. No lion shall be there, nor any ravenous beast shall

WHEN THE KING COMES BACK

go up thereon, it shall not be found there; but the redeemed shall walk there:

"And the ransomed of the Lord shall return, and come to Zion with songs and everlasting joy upon their head: and they shall obtain joy and gladness, and sorrow and sighing shall flee away."

In these ten verses we have another of Isaiah's greatest and most wonderful prophecies, not about the Church, but about Israel and the Promised Land. Here the prophet soars to the highest heights in describing the glories of the millennium. It almost sounds like the poetry of Heaven, or the songs of the angels. It is a scene, the like of which this old world has never seen.

Waste places are to become a Garden of Eden. Lands uninhabited will be populated. Deserts are to blossom and rejoice. I can imagine, from the sublime description, such rich and abundant vegetation, that the whole territory will be alive with the singing of birds and the joys of a plentiful harvest. Deserts will be gone. Waste places will produce.

No longer will the weak be weak, or the feeble feeble. No longer will the fearful be afraid. All will be strong and courageous. Fountains of water, never before discovered, will be found; and through lands where once there was nothing but sand, rivers will flow, bringing luxurious vegetation and an

WHEN ISAIAH SAW THE KING

abundance of everything. Parched ground will then be unknown.

That age, we are told, will be characterized by holiness. Highways, where once travellers were threatened by wild beasts, will now be safe. Sinners will not journey on them. No pollution of any kind will be encountered.

But language fails me. What a land! What a people! What a city! What a reign! Look now, as the ransomed of the Lord—with hearts overflowing with joy—turn their faces toward Jerusalem. Hear them as they sing their songs of gladness. Where, now, is their sorrow? Why no more sighs? "Sorrow and sighing," cries the prophet, have fled away. Only joy remains—"everlasting joy". Such are the indescribable blessings of the Kingdom Age.

COMFORT, JOY AND BLESSING

Turn to Isaiah 40: 1, 2:

"*Comfort ye, comfort ye my people, saith your God.*

"*Speak ye comfortably to Jerusalem, and cry unto her, that her warfare is accomplished, that her iniquity is pardoned: for she hath received of the Lord's hand double for all her sins.*"

Two thousand years have now passed and Jerusalem has at last become the capital of the new social

WHEN THE KING COMES BACK

order, for the kingdom of God has now been established on earth, and Jesus Christ is reigning on David's throne. Sin has been pardoned, suffering has ended, and all hearts are comforted. "And the glory of the Lord shall be revealed, and all flesh shall see it together" (vs. 5). No wonder the heart of the prophet sings for joy. Glory has taken the place of suffering, and comfort, that of sorrow.

See also Isaiah 40: 9–11:

"*O Zion, that bringest good tidings, get thee up into the high mountain; O Jerusalem, that bringest good tidings, lift up thy voice with strength; lift it up, be not afraid; say unto the cities of Judah, <u>Behold your God</u>!*

"<u>*Behold, the Lord God will come*</u> *with strong hand, and his arm shall rule for him: behold, his reward is with him, and his work before him.*

"*He shall feed his flock like a shepherd; he shall gather the lambs with his arm, and carry them in his bosom, and shall gently lead those that are with young.*"

Here is exaltation unspeakable and glory indescribable. Here is fearlessness and courage. Here is deity itself, the deity of Jesus Christ. "Behold your God" is the proclamation to the cities of Judah regarding the returned Messiah. Yes, Jesus is God. He is now in Jerusalem and the fact is heralded far and wide. For the Golden Age has been ushered in, the millennium has been established.

WHEN ISAIAH SAW THE KING

He comes. He rules. He rewards. He works. This is God's programme and it is now being fulfilled exactly as predicted. He nourishes His people, defends the weak, protects the helpless, and provides for all. "He shall bring forth judgment to the Gentiles" (chapter 41: 1). "He shall not fail nor be discouraged, till he have set judgment in the earth: and the isles shall wait for his law" (chapter 42: 4). Not only will He govern regathered Israel, He will also rule over the Gentiles. All nations will bow before Him. Even the most distant isle will obey His law. He will be the Supreme Ruler of all the world.

All Israel will be gathered and settled in the land of Palestine. "Fear not: for I am with thee: I will bring thy seed from the east, and gather thee from the west; I will say to the north, Give up; and to the south, Keep not back: bring my sons from far, and my daughters from the ends of the earth" (43: 5, 6). "Behold, these shall come from far: and, lo these from the north and from the west; and these from the land of Sinim" (49: 12).

"For a small moment have I forsaken thee; but with great mercies will I gather thee. In a little wrath I hid my face from thee for a moment; but with everlasting kindness will I have mercy on thee, saith the Lord thy Redeemer."—Isa. 54: 7, 8.

"Surely the isles shall wait for me, and the ships

WHEN THE KING COMES BACK

of Tarshish first, to bring thy sons from far, their silver and their gold with them, unto the name of the Lord thy God, and to the Holy One of Israel, because he hath glorified thee."—Isa. 60: 9.

HEARTS FILLED WITH GLADNESS

Let us look at Isaiah 51: 3:

"For the Lord shall comfort Zion: he will comfort all her waste places; and he will make her wilderness like Eden, and her desert like the garden of the Lord; joy and gladness shall be found therein, thanksgiving and the voice of melody."

Jerusalem is to become a city of comfort. For three thousand years it has been a city of suffering, war, bloodshed and sorrow. Oh, what a change! The wilderness that has surrounded the city of Jerusalem now becomes a Garden of Eden. No more desolation, no more barren rocks and drifting sand. Instead, the garden of the Lord.

Joy and gladness fill the hearts of her people. Songs, the like of which they never sang before, are now sung. All hearts are full of praise and thanksgiving. Oh, what a prospect! "Therefore the redeemed of the Lord shall return, and come with singing unto Zion; and everlasting joy shall be upon their head: they shall obtain gladness and joy; and sorrow and mourning shall flee away"

WHEN ISAIAH SAW THE KING

(51: 11). God has now comforted His people (51: 12).

So now the prophet calls upon her to awaken, for the time has come for her to be adorned with the beauty and glory of the Lord. "Awake, awake; put on thy strength, O Zion; put on thy beautiful garments, O Jerusalem, the holy city" (52: 1). "Thy God reigneth!" is now the proclamation (52: 7). Yes, He reigns at Jerusalem, the Lord Jesus Christ, and He is God.

JOY IN ZION

Turn to Isaiah 52: 9, 10, 13:

"Break forth into joy, sing together, ye waste places of Jerusalem: for the Lord hath comforted his people, he hath redeemed Jerusalem. The Lord hath made bare his holy arm in the eyes of all the nations; and all the ends of the earth shall see the salvation of our God."

Was ever such joy known before? Not in six thousand known years of man's history. The millennium has now been ushered in. God has made known His power. All the nations of the world have seen His glory. And now all is joy and gladness. Waste and desert places become beautiful. Zion has been redeemed, and Jesus Christ is now exalted and extolled. He has become the greatest of the great, and the highest of the high (52: 13).

WHEN THE KING COMES BACK

LIGHT AT LAST

Let us read Isaiah 59: 20:

"And the Redeemer shall come to Zion, and unto them that turn from transgression in Jacob, saith the Lord."

Now comes the question, When will Christ return? When will the Redeemer come to Zion? That He will come there can be no doubt. This very passage says that He will. But when will He appear? That is the question.

Paul tells us that it will be when the Church has been completed, when the Gentiles, who are to make up the Church have been saved (Rom. 11: 23–29). James says that it will be when God has taken out from among the Gentile nations a people for His name (Acts 15: 14–17). Hence this glorious prediction was not fulfilled when He came the first time. It has to do with His Second Advent—when He comes again. Therefore, we hear the prophet exclaiming:

"Arise, shine; for thy light is come, and the glory of the Lord is risen upon thee. For, behold, the darkness shall cover the earth, and gross darkness the people: but the Lord shall arise upon thee, and his glory shall be seen upon thee."—Isa. 60: 1, 2.

WHEN ISAIAH SAW THE KING

NEITHER VIOLENCE NOR DESTRUCTION

Here we read Isaiah 60: 18-20:

"Violence shall no more be heard in thy land, wasting nor destruction within thy borders; but thou shalt call thy walls Salvation, and thy gates Praise. The sun shall be no more thy light by day; neither for brightness shall the moon give light unto thee: but the Lord shall be unto thee an everlasting light, and thy God thy glory. The sun shall no more go down; neither shall thy moon withdraw itself: for the Lord shall be thine everlasting light, and the days of thy mourning shall be ended."

Violence—how God hates it! How every true Christian hates it, too! Robbery with violence, what a crime! Surely the death penalty would not be too severe a sentence.

Destruction—will the world ever see its end? Think of the bombed cities of Europe, the waste and destruction in Korea, the rape of Poland. Man destroys, and he destroys by violence. Will there ever, we ask—will there ever be a change?

Thank God, there will. Violence will be gone, destruction will be no more, and waste never again be known. Walls will be called Salvation, and gates Praise. In that day God will be the light and glory of His people, and the days of mourning will be ended. Oh, what a day!

WHEN THE KING COMES BACK

Are we going to spiritualize it, or do we actually want and expect it to take place? I believe that when Jesus comes again to take over the reins of government it will all be realized. The very earth itself will be glorified. In that day, says Isaiah, "They shall build the old wastes, they shall raise up the former desolations, and they shall repair the waste cities, the desolations of many generations" (61: 4). Jerusalem, the holy city, will yet be made a praise in the earth (Isa. 62: 1, 6, 7).

CHRIST IN ZION

Let us turn now to Isaiah 65: 17–25:

"Behold, I create new heavens and a new earth: and the former shall not be remembered, nor come into mind. But be ye glad and rejoice for ever in that which I create: for, behold, I create Jerusalem a rejoicing, and her people a joy. And I will rejoice in Jerusalem, and joy in my people: and the voice of weeping shall be no more heard in her, nor the voice of crying.

"There shall be no more thence an infant of days, nor an old man that hath not filled his days; for the child shall die an hundred years old; but the sinner being an hundred years old shall be accursed.

"And they shall build houses, and inhabit them; and they shall plant vineyards, and eat the fruit of

WHEN ISAIAH SAW THE KING

them. They shall not build, and another inhabit; they shall not plant, and another eat: for as the days of a tree are the days of my people, and mine elect shall long enjoy the work of their hands. They shall not labour in vain, nor bring forth for trouble; for they are the seed of the blessed of the Lord, and their offspring with them.

"And it shall come to pass, that before they call, I will answer; and while they are yet speaking, I will hear. The wolf and the lamb shall feed together, and the lion shall eat straw like the bullock: and dust shall be the serpent's meat. They shall not hurt nor destroy in all my holy mountain, said the Lord."

What a glorious prophecy! The Golden Age has come. Christ reigns in Zion. Joy now characterizes the people of Jerusalem, and the Lord Himself rejoices. All weeping has ceased. Tears no longer flow. The sob of a million heartaches is hushed forever. No more weeping. No more crying. Anguish and agony are felt no more.

<u>Longevity, like that before the flood, will be restored</u>. Life has been so short. It used to be long. Man scarcely begins to live until he must die. There is so much he wants to accomplish, but there is so little time. Now, at last, he will be able to live and enjoy the work of his hands. Old men will be numerous and they will seem young. If they die at a hundred, they will be looked upon as children. It

WHEN THE KING COMES BACK

will then pay to take time to build, for men will build for hundreds of years to come. They will live to rejoice and enjoy the fruit of their labours. So long will they live that God compares them to trees and says that the life of a man, in that day, will be as the life of a tree.

Now, again, we have the prediction about the wolf, the lamb, and the lion. They dwell together. Their appetites are changed. No longer are they meat-eating animals. They now exist on vegetation. Harmony prevails on every side. All is peace, not only among men, but also among animals. No longer do they hurt each other. "They shall not hurt nor destroy in all my holy mountain, saith the Lord." Perfect security in the kingdom of God on earth. Such is the prophet's picture of this world of ours during the millennial reign of Christ.

And in that day, as pictured here—not during the days of the Great Tribulation, but in the thousand years of kingdom blessedness—Israel will declare the glory of their Messiah among the Gentile nations of the world (Isa. 66: 19). The wicked will be destroyed and the Lord alone worshipped (66: 23, 24). Such is Isaiah's picture of the Kingdom Age.

CHAPTER 5

WHEN JEREMIAH SAW THE KINGDOM AGE

JEREMIAH is known as the weeping prophet; yet he wrote of the Kingdom Age, an age not yet born. Where did he get his information? From God. God knows the end from the beginning and He calls it prophecy. Prophecy is history written in advance. In the midst of his awful persecutions and horrible sufferings, Jeremiah gives us a picture of the glories of the coming kingdom, and his predictions agree with all the others, though he lived in another generation, for they came from God.

Jeremiah is the prophet of gloom and judgment. He predicts the destruction of Jerusalem and the scattering of the Jewish people among the nations. (See Jeremiah 9: 11, 16; 13: 19; 21: 10). All this was literally fulfilled. But then, too, he speaks of the regathering of the people and their ultimate glory. This also will be just as literally fulfilled. (See Jeremiah 16: 14-16; 23: 7, 8.)

WHEN THE KING COMES BACK

ISRAEL AND JUDAH RETURN

In Jeremiah 30: 3 we have a very clear and emphatic statement. It reads as follows:

"For, lo, the days come, saith the Lord, that I will bring again the captivity of my people Israel and Judah, saith the Lord: and I will cause them to return to the land that I gave to their fathers, and they shall possess it."

Some two thousand five hundred years have gone by since God made that prediction and it has not yet been fulfilled. But just as surely as day follows night, it will be. The days will come, the days of which He speaks.

It was not fulfilled after the seventy years' captivity, when the Jews returned from Babylon, for at that time the Northern kingdom did not return. As a matter of fact, only a few of the Babylonian captives came back; the bulk of the nation remained in exile.

Nor has it been fulfilled in the return of the Jews in this twentieth century. Again only some of those of the tribe of Judah have gone back. Israel is still in exile. Moreover, they have not by any means inherited the entire land, and according to God's programme, all others are to be driven out and they alone are to possess it. In this very verse it states that they are to possess the land of their fathers and

WHEN JEREMIAH SAW THE KINGDOM AGE

I take it that that means the whole land. This they have never done. Only when they do will this prediction be fulfilled.

However, the time is coming when the days of which the Lord speaks in this prophecy will actually be here. Both Israel and Judah, all twelve tribes, will return to the land of their fathers and will possess it. But it will not be the work of politicians; God Himself will bring it about. This amazing prophecy has yet to be fulfilled.

THE GLORIES OF THE KINGDOM

Turn now to Jeremiah 23: 5, 6:

"Behold, the days come, saith the Lord, that I will raise unto David a righteous Branch, and a King shall reign and prosper, and shall execute judgment and justice in the earth. In his days Judah shall be saved, and Israel shall dwell safely: and this is his name whereby he shall be called, THE LORD OUR RIGHTEOUSNESS."

We come now to the glories of the kingdom. Again we are introduced to the Branch. He is of the line of David. He is a King. He reigns and prospers, and He executes judgment and justice in the earth. Not in Heaven, mark you, but right here on earth. Who is He? He is Christ the Messiah.

During the days of His reign, Judah and Israel

WHEN THE KING COMES BACK

are united and saved. At long last they dwell together, safe and secure. He is known as "THE LORD OF OUR RIGHTEOUSNESS." Was this amazing prophecy fulfilled at the time of the first advent? It was not—none of it. It will be fulfilled when He comes again; the time is still future.

After speaking of the Great Tribulation, "Jacob's Trouble" (Jer. 30: 5–7), the prophet tells of a day that follows when the people will serve "David their king," who will again appear, the Lord Jesus Christ, so often referred to as "David", when He comes again (Jer. 30: 9).

DAVID THEIR KING

Let us read Jeremiah 30: 10, 11:

"Therefore fear thou not, O my servant Jacob, saith the Lord; neither be dismayed, O Israel: for, lo, I will save thee from afar, and thy seed from the land of their captivity; and Jacob shall return, and shall be in rest, and be quiet, and none shall make him afraid. For I am with thee, saith the Lord, to save thee: though I make a full end of all nations whither I have scattered thee, yet will I not make a full end of thee."

When Christ, "David their king", has been raised up to govern them, they will never have reason to fear again. They will return from all the countries

WHEN JEREMIAH SAW THE KINGDOM AGE

of the world and dwell in their own land once more. There they will be at rest. There they will be quiet. Other nations have and will perish; they will remain. The Jewish nation will never disappear (Jer. 46: 27, 28). Neither Hitler, nor anyone else, will ever be able to annihilate them.

Look at Jeremiah 31: 33, 34:

"After those days, saith the Lord, I will put my law in their inward parts, and write it in their hearts; and will be their God, and they shall be my people. And they shall teach no more every man his neighbour, and every man his brother, saying, Know the Lord: for they shall all know me, from the least of them unto the greatest of them, saith the Lord: for I will forgive their iniquity, and I will remember their sin no more."

The old relationship between God and His people is again re-established. But now they do not obey because they are commanded to, but because they want to. God's law is no longer on tables of stone; it is now in their hearts.

UNIVERSAL SALVATION

Here then, at last, is universal salvation—an entire nation obedient to God. All now "know Him", old and young alike. No longer is it necessary to send out teachers and preachers to instruct the

WHEN THE KING COMES BACK

people; all have already been reached; all have a knowledge of God. Israel has at last been forgiven.

Note Jeremiah 32: 37–41:

"Behold, I will gather them out of all countries, whither I have driven them in mine anger, and in my fury, and in great wrath; and I will bring them again unto this place, and I will cause them to dwell safely: And they shall be my people, and I will be their God:

"And I will give them one heart, and one way, that they may fear me for ever, for the good of them, and of their children after them: And I will make an everlasting covenant with them, that I will not turn away from them, to do them good; but I will put my fear in their hearts, that they shall not depart from me. Yea, I will rejoice over them to do them good, and I will plant them in this land assuredly with my whole heart and with my whole soul."

God drove them out. God will bring them back. They were dispersed throughout all countries; they will be brought back to one. There they will be safe. God now becomes their God and they become His people. So completely does God possess their hearts that they now fear, love and serve Him perfectly, and never will they want to leave Him again. He settles them in the land of Palestine and rejoices over them with great joy. His wrath against them has subsided and His great purpose has been accomplished.

WHEN JEREMIAH SAW THE KINGDOM AGE

THE BRANCH OF RIGHTEOUSNESS

See Jeremiah 33: 15-17:

"In those days, and at that time, will I cause the Branch of righteousness to grow up unto David; and he shall execute judgment and righteousness in the land. In those days shall Judah be saved, and Jerusalem shall dwell safely: and this is the name wherewith she shall be called, The Lord our righteousness. For thus saith the Lord; David shall never want a man to sit upon the throne of the house of Israel."

I have chosen to quote these three verses, but I should like to quote the whole chapter, for chapter 33 presents a complete picture of the Davidic Kingdom of the future. It is one of Jeremiah's greatest prophecies and every verse in it is important. Read it. Read of the joy of that day. Read of the glories of the Golden Age.

Here again is the Branch, the glorified, reigning Messiah, Jesus Christ. He rules over Israel and executes judgment and justice on every side. "David shall never want a man to sit upon the throne of the house of Israel," said God. But, unless David's greater Son, the Lord Jesus Christ, comes back to occupy that throne, this prediction can never be fulfilled. Make no mistake—He is coming back. He will rule. Verses 19 to 26 prove it. Christ is Victor. He must reign as King.

WHEN THE KING COMES BACK

Do you know that Christ will come again some day
    To receive His Bride, His own,
And to reign on earth for a thousand years
    As the King of David's throne?

Do you know that we shall share that wondrous reign
    If we suffer with Him here,
If we bear the cross in this world of woe
    With our Lord we shall appear?

Do you know that righteousness will flourish then,
    And that war will be no more,
For the Prince of Peace will Himself be King,
    And the reign of sin be o'er?

—O.J.S.

CHAPTER 6

WHEN EZEKIEL SAW THE KING

EZEKIEL, like all the other prophets, writes of the dispersion, the restoration and the glory of the children of Israel under the future reign of Christ, none of which was fulfilled at the first advent. Two thousand five hundred years have now gone by and it is still future. All await the coming of Christ and the establishment of His kingdom on earth. <u>In that day there will be a literal fulfilment of every prediction he ever made</u>.

THEIR HEARTS WILL BE CHANGED

Turn to <u>Ezekiel 11: 17-20</u>:

"Therefore say, Thus saith the Lord God; I will even gather you from the people, and assemble you out of the countries where ye have been scattered, and <u>I will give you the land of Israel</u>. And I will give them one heart, and I will put a new spirit within you; and I will take the stony heart out of their flesh, and will give them an heart of flesh: That they may walk in my statutes, and keep mine ordin-

WHEN THE KING COMES BACK

ances, and do them: and they shall be my people, and I will be their God."

Israel, now dispersed, is to be regathered from all the countries of the world and restored to the land of Palestine.

When that great event takes place, their very hearts will be changed. Hearts that are now bitter and hard will be made soft. Such is not the condition of the Jews who, in their unbelief and hardness of heart, are now returning to Palestine.

At that time God will fill them with His Spirit and they will be utterly changed. Today they hate the very name of Jesus; then they will love it. Not until then will they walk in the ways of the Lord and do His will. Only then will they become His people and will He be their God.

THEY WILL BE SECURE

Let us read Ezekiel 34: 23-30:

"And I will set up one shepherd over them, and he shall feed them, even my servant David; he shall feed them, and he shall be their shepherd. And I the Lord will be their God, and my servant David a prince among them; I the Lord have spoken it.

"And I will make with them a covenant of peace, and will cause the evil beasts to cease out of the land: and they shall dwell safely in the wilderness, and

WHEN EZEKIEL SAW THE KING

sleep in the woods. And I will make them and the places round about my hill a blessing; and I will cause the shower to come down in his season; there shall be showers of blessing.

"And the tree of the field shall yield her fruit, and the earth shall yield her increase, and they shall be safe in their land, and shall know that I am the Lord, when I have broken the bands of their yoke, and delivered them out of the hand of those that served themselves of them. And they shall <u>no more be a prey to the heathen</u>, neither shall the beast of the land devour them; but they shall dwell safely, and none shall make them afraid.

"And I will raise up for them a plant of renown, and they shall be no more consumed with hunger in the land, neither bear the shame of the heathen any more. Thus shall they know that I the Lord their God am with them, and that they, even the house of Israel, are my people, saith the Lord God."

CHRIST WILL BE THEIR PRINCE

After drawing a beautiful picture of a regathered and restored Israel (Ezek. 34: 11–16), in language similar to that of the other prophets, Ezekiel goes on to describe the blessing and security of Israel under David, their Shepherd. That one Shepherd is Christ, the greater David. He will be their Prince.

WHEN THE KING COMES BACK

Peace will be the chief characteristic of that new day; peace the like of which the world has never known before, a peace that never again will be broken. Wild beasts will be tame. The wilderness will be as safe as the village. To lie down and sleep in the woods will be perfectly safe. Rain will be plentiful. "There shall be showers of blessing." An abundant harvest will result. Fruit trees will be loaded. Famine and hunger will be unknown.

<u>Nothing of this took place after the return from Babylon</u>. It will all be realized when the King comes back to reign. This is millenniel blessing. God speed the day!

THEY WILL BE CLEANSED BY THE SPIRIT

Turn to Ezekiel <u>36: 23-38</u>:

"The heathen shall know that I am the Lord, saith the Lord God, when I shall be sanctified in you before their eyes. For I will take you from among the heathen, and gather you out of all countries, and will bring you into your own land.

"Then will I sprinkle clean water upon you, and ye shall be clean: from all your filthiness, and from all your idols, will I cleanse you. A new heart also will I give you, and a new spirit will I put within you: and I will take away the stony heart out of your flesh, and I will give you an heart of flesh. And I

WHEN EZEKIEL SAW THE KING

will put my spirit within you, and cause you to walk in my statutes, and ye shall keep my judgments, and do them.

"And ye shall dwell in the land that I gave to your fathers; and ye shall be my people, and I will be your God. I will also save you from all your uncleannesses: and I will call for the corn, and will increase it, and lay no famine upon you. And I will multiply the fruit of the tree, and the increase of the field, that ye shall receive no more reproach of famine among the heathen. Then shall ye remember your own evil ways, and your doings that were not good, and shall loathe yourselves in your own sight for your iniquities and for your abominations. Not for your sakes do I this, saith the Lord God, be it known unto you: be ashamed and confounded for your own ways, O house of Israel.

"Thus saith the Lord God; In the day that I shall have cleansed you from all your iniquities I will also cause you to dwell in the cities, and the wastes shall be builded. And the desolate land shall be tilled, whereas it lay desolate in the sight of all that passed by. And they shall say, This land that was desolate is become like the garden of Eden; and the waste and desolate and ruined cities are become fenced, and are inhabited. Then the heathen that are left round about you shall know that I the Lord build the ruined places, and plant that that was desolate: I the Lord have spoken it, and I will do it.

WHEN THE KING COMES BACK

"Thus saith the Lord God; <u>I will yet for this be enquired of by the house of Israel, to do it for them;</u> I will increase them with men like a flock. As the holy flock, as the flock of Jerusalem in her solemn feasts; so shall the waste cities be filled with flocks of men: and they shall know that I am the Lord."

THEY WILL BE A BLESSING

<u>Israel will never be a blessing to the world until they have been restored to their own land</u>. So here again is the repeated prediction of the regathering and conversion of God's people. When Christ returns and the millennium dawns, Israel will be given a new heart and a new spirit, and will become obedient.

No greater prophecy has ever been given than this. Much that the other prophets reveal is here repeated and emphasized. It speaks of the heart-cleansing that will follow the restoration. Then, again, it tells of a day when there will be an abundance of everything, when famine will be unknown. No need then of taxes. That vicious system that makes so many of the honest dishonest will be gone and gone forever. There will be no need, for the earth at last will yield its increase. The curse will be lifted. What a picture of prosperity. Waste and desolate places are now inhabited. The word "depression" has at last disappeared from the

WHEN EZEKIEL SAW THE KING

vocabulary of the human race. The population of the world will be enormously increased, and the whole land will become a Garden of Eden.

My friend, read this prophecy again. Every verse is a new revelation. Is it conceivable that it could be spiritualized? Or was it fulfilled at the time of the first advent? Is there any other way to interpret it except as it reads? How can it be understood unless it means just what it says? The fulfilment must be literal. It is a picture of the glories of Israel during the reign of Christ. This is millennial blessing. This is the Golden Age. This is the kingdom of God on earth. Israel has been regathered and converted. Iniquity has been purged away and hearts cleansed. Poverty is a thing of the past. Labour is light and fruitful. God is at last exalted and glorified. Palestine has become the most beautiful land in the world, and Israel the most favoured nation. Repentance will be genuine and humility real.

This then is the picture drawn by Ezekiel. This is God's revelation to His prophet. It is a prediction that will actually come to pass right here on earth. Beautiful is the description, glorious the vision. This is the transfiguration continued for a thousand years. Jesus Christ is now King of kings and Lord of lords. Once he trod the dirt roads of earth, lowly and despised; now He is reigning on David's throne in millennial power and splendour. How we long for it!

WHEN THE KING COMES BACK

No wonder John prayed, "Even so, come; Lord Jesus."

ISRAEL WILL BE REVIVED

Our passage here is Ezekiel chapter 37. Study it carefully. I am not going to quote it verbatim. It describes the revival that will take place in the nation of Israel when God brings them out of their graves among the nations, and they live again. It speaks of two sticks, Judah and Israel, and predicts that they will become one again. It portrays both a regathering and a restoration, followed by personal and national cleansing.

"David my servant shall be king over them; and they all shall have one shepherd: they shall also walk in my judgments, and observe my statutes, and do them. And they shall dwell in the land that I have given unto Jacob my servant, wherein your fathers have dwelt; and they shall dwell therein, even they, and their children, and their children's children for ever: and my servant David shall be their prince for ever."—Ezek. 37: 24, 25.

This needs no explanation. It is perfectly clear. Jesus Christ, here called David, is their Ruler. Israel is back in her own land. It is a time of peace. They multiply as never before, and God is in their midst. This is the picture of Ezekiel chapter 37. What a glorious prophecy of the age that is to be!

CHAPTER 7

WHEN DANIEL SAW THE KINGDOM

NO PROPHET has ever given such a practical forecast of the King and the kingdom as Daniel. Some six hundred years before Christ, he wrote of His coming. Two thousand five hundred years have now gone by and his greatest predictions still await fulfilment.

Many of the prophets wrote of Christ's humiliation, His sufferings, and His death. Daniel wrote of the King in His beauty, His glory, His exaltation. Daniel saw Him enthroned—a world ruler, supreme over all. That day is yet to come. Not until all other kingdoms have been overthrown will it be realized.

<u>Have you ever noticed how often the words "King," "kingdom," "rule," "govern," "throne," are used in the Book of Daniel</u>? Count them, if you will, and you will be amazed. Daniel is the Book of the King and His kingdom. Earthly kingdoms are discussed and set aside. All culminates in the rule of Jesus Christ, who is to sit on David's throne and govern the entire world. All nations, kings, and potentates are to bow before Him, for He is to be

WHEN THE KING COMES BACK

Lord of lords and King of kings. As a matter of fact, He is spoken of in Revelation 1: 5 as "the Prince of the kings of the earth". Hence, He is to rule over all other kings.

WORLD POWERS DESTROYED

First of all, see Daniel 2: 44:

"And in the days of these kings shall the God of heaven set up a kingdom, which shall never be destroyed: and the kingdom shall not be left to other people, but it shall break in pieces and consume all these kingdoms, and it shall stand for ever."

This is the vision that describes the sudden destruction of the last great world power. It is not gradual; it is sudden. Christ is a smiting stone. The present world systems are to be destroyed. Those who look for world conversion are totally ignorant of the meaning of this vision. Christ's kingdom fills the whole earth *only* after the smiting. It is worldwide in its dominion and influence.

But let us go back a little. You remember the vision as seen by King Nebuchadnezzar. "Thou, O king, sawest, and behold a great image . . . This image's head was of fine gold, his breast and his arms of silver, his belly and his thighs of brass, His legs of iron, his feet part of iron and part of clay" (Dan. 2: 31–33).

WHEN DANIEL SAW THE KINGDOM

The gold, you will remember, represented Babylon, the first great world power; the silver, the next great empire, Media-Persia; the brass, Greece; and the iron, Rome. All of them were world empires, and they appeared in that order, exactly as foretold.

Then the king saw a stone, cut out of the mountain with hands, crash into the feet of the image and grind it to powder. God was making known to the king, Daniel said, what was to come to pass. Already the four world powers have appeared. Rome disintegrated, but the fragments still remain. <u>Out of the present world systems will come ten nations represented by the ten toes, and then the Stone will strike.</u>

That, then, will be the next great event in world history. Soon now will come the crushing blow that will demolish all world powers. With the appearing of Jesus Christ in millennial power and glory, as Lord of lords and King of kings, will come the complete and final overthrow of all earthly governments, powers and dominions.

WHEN WILL IT TAKE PLACE?

<u>Not one word of this prediction was fulfilled at the first advent.</u> The world powers were not destroyed. They never have been destroyed, nor will they be until Christ, the Smiting Stone, at a single

WHEN THE KING COMES BACK

stroke, demolishes them all. It will be judgment, sudden and final. The fatal blow was not struck when He came the first time. Then the world struck Him. When this happens He will do the striking. It will be a startling and world shaking catastrophe and, immediately after, the kingdom of God will be established on earth.

When will it be? "In the days of these things." Never yet have they been seen. <u>The revived Roman Empire has yet to be ruled by ten dictators</u>. When that day comes the Stone will strike, and not until then. That is the direction in which we are now headed. Ten men will finally rule the world. When that day dawns, judgment will fall. Christ will come. At a single stroke all ten will be overthrown and destroyed. No dictator will survive. All are doomed.

"In the days of these kings shall the God of heaven set up a kingdom." Man does not bring in the kingdom. The Church does not do it. <u>All this talk about co-operatives, church union, a world church—all such talk is nothing but trash</u>. It is absolutely contradictory to the precepts of the Word of God. The Devil himself would sanction a world church. The synagogue of Satan is already in the making. <u>And all who are working for a world church are working for the enemy</u>. No, my friend, God Himself is to usher in the kingdom.

This is not the spiritual kingdom in which we

WHEN DANIEL SAW THE KINGDOM

all believe; it is a literal kingdom right here on earth, established after the striking of a single blow, as if by a hydrogen bomb, world-wide in its destruction. This is the kingdom described by the prophets—the glorious reign of Christ.

A UNIVERSAL KINGDOM

Next, Daniel 7: 27:

"And the kingdom and dominion, and the greatness of the kingdom under the whole heaven, shall be given to the people of the saints of the most High, whose kingdom is an everlasting kingdom, and all dominions shall serve and obey him."

This is a different vision, but of the same kingdom. It is to be established "under the whole heaven". No kingdom has ever been so great, so magnificent, so powerful. It will be governed under Christ by the people of God. All nations will bow down and obey Him. Hence it will be universal. He, the Lord Jesus Christ, will be the supreme Ruler, for the mountain of His kingdom is to fill all the earth. What a day that will be! This is man's day; God's day is coming.

Today the nations, like beasts of prey, rule and govern by force. War after war has been fought. Oh, the blood that man has shed! Man's inhumanity to

WHEN THE KING COMES BACK

man—who can describe it?! Russia's concentration camps, where millions of human slaves are worked and beaten to death, or shot; where life is cheap and brute force dominates—what a ghastly system! Never in the six thousand years of man's history has there been such a diabolic dictatorship. Cruelty, brutality and violence are its chief characteristics. Truth it does not know. Lies and hypocrisy dominate it. Black slavery was a paradise in comparison. No such bloodthirsty tyrant has ever appeared. Millions have perished. Other millions will be murdered, for it knows no mercy. Atheism is its creed. It would tear God Himself out of His Heaven. And yet there are ministers who advocate it, even though they know they would be the first to die. Communism is atheism. Hence, no one—Mohammedan, Christian or Jew—who believes in God, can be a communist.

So terrible is it that, when American soldiers tried to send refugees back to Russia, because of the inhuman and shameful Yalta agreement, they fought with teeth and nails in a wild and desperate effort to escape, willing rather to die than return. And, when their writers were told to say more about the joys of Russian life, they answered by pointing out that millions had just buried those who had died from planned famine. Millions more, they said, were in jails and concentration camps, where they were

WHEN DANIEL SAW THE KINGDOM

perishing from cold, torture and starvation. Of the thousands who returned to the "Soviet Paradise", most were murdered or tortured to death in a slave camp. Few, if any, survived.

Will the world ever forget the frightful man-made famine when Stalin collected grain by force and more than four million people died, while another fifteen million were killed and other millions were sent to Siberia and the Arctic regions? Or the great purge when fifty thousand were executed and hundreds of thousands forced into slave labour camps? When the war broke out, a million Russians put on German uniforms in the desperate hope of escaping. When they were forced back, hundreds committed suicide rather than return to the horrors of communism.

Between 1950 and 1952, the communists executed two hundred Chinese a day in Shanghai alone, according to a Reuter dispatch. British estimates put the executions in China at 14 million, a very conservative figure. What wholesale murder! God help them when they appear before the Great White Throne!

No civilized government obtains confessions by force. Only the most hardened pagans and criminals use such tactics. Among civilized nations a man is considered innocent until he is proved guilty. Not even his own confession of guilt is sufficient to con-

WHEN THE KING COMES BACK

demn him without evidence. Communism uses the third degree, namely: physical torture, to compel innocent men and women to confess, and then condemns them on the basis of their own confession. Even savages would not stoop so low. In my mind the third degree is the greatest of all crimes and should be punished with death. In Russia and China millions of innocent men and women have undergone the most brutal physical and mental torture to force them to confess to something of which they were not guilty, and tens of thousands have died under the inhuman sufferings inflicted upon them by those monsters of cruelty who, some day, must themselves face the judgment of God.

Well, now, contrast this brutal system with the glorious kingdom of God, when love will govern and peace reign. What a change will take place. And of this change Daniel and the prophets write. <u>No wonder the Devil hates prophecy</u>. Justice, the Bible says, will then be meted out. Righteousness will flourish. Violence, cruelty and brutality will be gone. There will be no more pain, no more suffering, no more slavery. All men will be free. Life will be safe and secure and none will go hungry again.

WHEN DANIEL SAW THE KINGDOM

CHRIST IS VICTOR

Now Daniel 7: 14:

"And there was given him dominion, and glory, and a kingdom, that all people, nations, and languages, should serve him: his dominion is an everlasting dominion, which shall not pass away, and his kingdom that which shall not be destroyed."

Christ is Victor! Here it is in Daniel 7: 14. "There was given him dominion." Hence, He reigns. He is King. He has a kingdom over which He rules, and it is a glorious kingdom. What the three disciples saw in a few moments on the Mount of Transfiguration, we now see for a thousand years on all the earth, for His kingdom covers the entire globe.

All peoples serve Him. All nations submit to His rule. All languages acknowledge Him. His reign is universal, His kingdom world-wide. The Eskimo in the Arctic, the Indians of the jungles, the Arabs of the desert, the Tibetans on the roof of the world, China's teeming millions, and India's countless multitudes, obey His edicts and commands. Never has a ruler had such a following. No such kingdom has ever existed.

It will be strong, because He is strong. All Heaven will be back of it—all the power of God Himself. Satan will be impotent, for he will be in

WHEN THE KING COMES BACK

chains, securely bound. He can do nothing. No world power will ever rise against it. It will be safe from destruction.

It will need no armies or navies for its defence. No hydrogen bombs will be used to protect it against aggression. Soldiers and armaments will be no more. Never again will young men be conscripted for the army, there to be taught to drink and debauch themselves, there to lose their purity and their virtue. No longer will they leave multitudes of nameless babies in the lands they conquer. No longer will young women be robbed of their virtue and ruined for life. Rape and loot, drunkenness and brutality, waste and desolation and sorrow—the harvest of every war—will be no more. Nothing but the kingdom of Christ can end it all. No one but Jesus Himself can usher in the Golden Age, and rule without an army.

Hear now God's last word to Daniel: "But go thou thy way till the end be: for thou shalt rest, and stand in thy lot at the end of the days" (Dan. 12:13). When it is all over, Daniel will be there. He will be a witness to it. He will see his visions fulfilled to the letter. What a day that will be, the day when the King comes back to reign!

CHAPTER 8

WHEN THE PSALMIST SAW THE KING

LET US TURN now to the Psalms of David. Let us see what he can tell us about the King and His kingdom. We will find that he had a great deal to say about the sufferings of Christ and His future glory. Jesus, you remember, told His disciples that there were many prophecies written about Him in the Psalms (Luke 24: 44).

First, Psalm 2: 6:

"*Yet have I set my king upon my holy hill of Zion.*"

The entire Psalm is Messianic. The heathen rage. Kings and rulers take counsel together. They would tear God from His throne in Heaven, fools that they are. What a picture of communism! But God can afford to laugh at them in their impotence, and, when He is ready, pour out His wrath upon them, for, in spite of all they can do, Jesus Christ will be enthroned at Jerusalem, and all nations will bow to His authority. The heathen will become His inheritance and the uttermost part of the earth His possession. He will rule them with a rod of iron and instantly judge the rebellious.

WHEN THE KING COMES BACK

HE SHALL HAVE DOMINION

Second, Psalm 22: 27, 28:

"*All the ends of the world shall remember and turn unto the Lord: and all the kindreds of the nations shall worship before thee. For the kingdom is the Lord's: and he is the governor among the nations.*"

While most of the Psalm deals with the first advent, these two verses refer to the second. All earth's inhabitants will turn to the Lord, not now, but when He comes again. Universal worship will then be His. Why? Because it is His kingdom that is to be set up and He, Jesus Christ, is to rule and govern the nations. The King of Glory has at last come into His own (Ps. 24: 7–10).

In Psalm 72 we have the most perfect picture of the Messiah and His glorious kingdom of the entire book. Jesus is King. He is to judge in righteousness. What a contrast to earth's rulers. "He shall judge thy people with righteousness, and thy poor with judgment." Nations large and small will be characterized by peace and righteousness during His reign. "The mountains shall bring peace to the people, and the little hills, by righteousness." Swift will be the judgment meted out on all oppressors. "He shall judge the poor of the people, he shall save the children of the needy, and shall break in pieces the oppressor." Today the wicked triumph.

WHEN THE PSALMIST SAW THE KING

Dictators oppress the people, but "in his days shall the righteous flourish." What a change!

"He shall have dominion also from sea to sea, and from the river unto the ends of the earth!" What a prediction! Oh, what a dominion! Christ at last is supreme. He reigns over the whole world. His rule is universal. Even in the lonely wilderness the natives submit to His rule, and His enemies everywhere are defeated. Kings and potentates bring Him presents and acknowledge His Kingship over them. "Yea, all kings shall fall down before him: all nations shall serve him." Hallelujah! What a Ruler!

"His name shall endure for ever . . . all nations shall call him blessed." Nebuchadnezzar, Alexander, Nero, Napoleon, Mussolini, Hitler, Stalin—all of them—earth's greatest rulers, have come and gone. Most of them have already been forgotten. But his name, the name of Jesus, will endure forever. The lowly carpenter of Nazareth, whom men crucified, is destined to become the supreme Ruler of the world, unequalled by any other. No wonder the Psalmist cries as he beholds the vision, "And let the whole earth be filled with his glory; Amen, and Amen." So be it and so let it be.

WHEN THE KING COMES BACK

THE GLORIES OF ZION

Last of all, Psalm 102: 13-16:

"Thou shalt arise, and have mercy upon Zion: for the time to favour her, yea, the set time, is come. For thy servants take pleasure in her stones, and favour the dust thereof. So the heathen shall fear the name of the Lord, and all the kings of the earth thy glory. When the Lord shall build up Zion, he shall appear in his glory."

There is a time appointed by God Himself for the restoration of His people and the glorification of Jerusalem. That time will surely come. For Jerusalem is to become the most wonderful city in all the world. In that day all the kings of earth will fear the glory of the Lord.

When will be the time? When will He rebuild and beautify Jerusalem? When He appears in Glory. At the time of His return to earth. When He comes back to reign as King on David's throne. Then, and not until then, will this great change take place. Then, and not until then, will Zion become God's city. But the time is coming when His purposes for Jerusalem will be carried out; for Zion is to be the capital of the great King, Jesus Christ. The Jews may try to rebuild the city now, but they will not succeed. Only the Messiah Himself is equal to the task.

WHEN THE PSALMIST SAW THE KING

No wonder the prophets sing of the glories of Zion during the millennium. "The Lord shall send the rod of thy strength out of Zion: rule thou in the midst of thine enemies" (Ps. 110: 2). And now, at long last, Revelation 11: 15 has been gloriously fulfilled: "The kingdoms of this world are become the kingdoms of our Lord, and of his Christ; and he shall reign for ever and ever." Thus will it be when the King comes back to reign.

But what, my friend, about you? Does Jesus Christ govern your life? Is there peace in your heart? Do you recognize Him as Lord of lords and King of kings? Does He reign in your soul? It is an individual matter, you see. You do not have to wait until the millennium to own your allegiance. You can acknowledge Him now.

Nineteen hundred years ago He died for you on Calvary's cross. Your sins were laid on Him. Now, all you have to do is to open your heart's closed door to Him and invite Him to come in.

You have sinned. The Bible says, "All have sinned" (Rom. 3: 23). Will you admit it? Then, if you have sinned, you are lost, and you need a Saviour. Do you know it? Moreover, you cannot save yourself. All your works, your religion, your goodness, will not avail in the least. You need a Saviour.

But, thank God, Jesus Christ can save you. He

WHEN THE KING COMES BACK

loved you enough to die for you. Your sins He bore in His own body on the tree. "The soul that sinneth it shall die," God says. But you do not have to die. Christ died that you might live. He has provided salvation for you. "It is finished," was His cry.

What then must you do? You must accept Him as your own personal Saviour. "As many as received him, to them gave he the power to become the sons of God" (John 1: 12). Water may be available, but you must drink it or you will still be thirsty. Food may be provided, but you must eat it or you will starve. Salvation is offered, but, unless you accept it, it will never be yours. A pardon must be received to be of value.

Well, now, will you choose Christ? You must make the decision. If you do, He will save you. You will be forgiven. You will have peace. Eternal life will be yours. But if you reject Him, you will perish. It is wonderful to have peace in the world, but it is still more wonderful to have peace in your heart. And that peace, my friend, may be yours right here and now, long before the coming of the millennium. Oh, then, let me beg of you to receive Jesus Christ this moment as your Lord and Saviour, and then you will be ready for the millennium. Will you do it? Do it, and do it NOW.

CHAPTER 9

WHEN THE APOSTLES SAW THE KINGDOM

THE NEW TESTAMENT, like the Old, speaks of the kingdom of God on earth. It too, predicts a literal millennium, a Golden Age, with Jesus Christ reigning as King. There is a spiritual kingdom and there is a physical kingdom, but the two are never confused. David's throne is yet to be established. "Thy kingdom come" is still the prayer of the Church.

Now for a vision of the glorified King. What will He be like? For that vision we turn to Matthew 17: 1–13. In the last verse of the previous chapter we are told that He is coming, but that when He comes this time it will be in His Kingdom; not to redeem but to rule; not in humiliation but in glory; not in the weakness of a babe but in the power of a King.

The Transfiguration actually took place, but it did not last. It was not intended to last; the time was not yet. It was but a glimpse of what His reign will be. Only Peter, James and John saw it. But

WHEN THE KING COMES BACK

they never forgot; they never could. Peter refers to it in his epistle.

A VISION OF THE KINGDOM

"For we have not followed cunningly devised fables, when we made known unto you the power and coming of our Lord Jesus Christ, but were eyewitnesses of his majesty. For he received from God the Father honour and glory, when there came such a voice to him from the excellent glory. This is my beloved Son, in whom I am well pleased. And this voice which came from heaven we heard, when we were with him in the holy mount."—2 Pet. 1: 16–18.

He speaks of the "power" of His coming and refers to Christ as "his majesty". He received, he says, "honour and glory", while the scene itself he describes as "the excellent glory".

Matthew says "his face did shine as the sun, and his raiment was white as the light". Think of it—"as the sun". How bright is the sun? Who can look at it? Yet the face of Jesus is still brighter. What a transfiguration! That is the way He will appear during the millennium.

His companions are heavenly beings, Moses and Elijah, and the voice is the voice of God. "This is my beloved Son, in whom I am well pleased; hear ye him." Elijah, He says, will precede His return.

WHEN THE APOSTLES SAW THE KINGDOM

John the Baptist could have been Elijah, had he been accepted, but he was not, and so Elijah himself is yet to come (Matt. 17: 10–13). "Behold, I will send you Elijah the prophet before the coming of the great and dreadful day of the Lord: And he shall turn the heart of the fathers to the children, and the heart of the children to their fathers, lest I come and smite the earth with a curse." (Mal. 4: 5, 6).

WHAT ABOUT THE APOSTLES?

In Matthew 19: 28, the kingdom is called "the regeneration". The word is only used in one other place in the entire Bible (Titus 3: 5), and there it has a purely spiritual significance. The Greek word is *paliggenesia* and it means to make over new, to recreate. Here the reference is to the coming kingdom when Jesus Christ will transform the entire social order.

Peter had asked the question, "Behold, we have forsaken all, and followed thee; what shall we have therefore?" In other words, "We have left our homes, our work, our friends, our all, and have followed Thee. That is the price we have paid. That is what it has cost us to become Thy disciples. Well, now, what are we going to get out of it? What is to be our reward?"

WHEN THE KING COMES BACK

It reminds us of the rich young ruler in Mark 10: 17–30, when Jesus said, "Sell whatsoever thou hast . . . and come, take up the cross and follow me." Now then, if a man does that, what will he get in return? That was Peter's question.

Let me paraphrase the answer of Jesus. "In the regeneration, when the Son of man shall sit in the throne of his glory, ye also shall sit upon twelve thrones, judging the twelve tribes of Israel, ye which have followed me."

Jesus is speaking of the millennium, the Golden Age, the thousand years reign, when He will be sitting on the throne of His father David. In other words, the Kingdom Age, when at last the long promised kingdom has come. During that period, He says, the twelve tribes of Israel will be governed by the twelve apostles. Each will be seated on a throne. It is to be a theocratic government as predicted in Isaiah 1: 26. That is to be their reward (Luke 22: 28–30).

But they were not satisfied, at least the two sons of Zebedee, James and John. Their mother wanted them to have the two chief seats of honour on His throne, the left, and the right. Having heard the kingdom was to become a reality and that the twelve apostles were to be chief rulers, she asked that her sons be given the places of honour nearest Him in His kingdom (Matt. 20: 20–28).

WHEN THE APOSTLES SAW THE KINGDOM

What was His answer? <u>Did he tell them that they were wrong, that there would not be a kingdom? Never</u>! He said such positions would be allotted in His kingdom, but that they would be given by His Father to those specially chosen.

WHEN WILL THE KINGDOM COME?

In Matthew 24 we have the order and means of the establishment of the kingdom of God on earth. The disciples wanted to know *the* sign of the end of the age. Christ first enumerates a number of signs, but adds, "the end is not yet. . . . All these are the beginning of sorrows". Then in verse 14, He mentions the sign that indicates the end, world evangelization, and adds, "then shall the end come".

Following that there is the Great Tribulation, and "immediately after" (vs. 29), His return to earth. It is not secret; it is spectacular. He compares it to the lightning. "For as the lightning cometh out of the east, and shineth even unto the west; so shall also the coming of the Son of man be."

"*Immediately after the tribulation of those days shall the sun be darkened, and the moon shall not give her light, and the stars shall fall from heaven, and the powers of the heavens shall be shaken:*

"*And then shall appear the sign of the Son of man in heaven: and then shall all the tribes of the earth*

WHEN THE KING COMES BACK

mourn, and they shall see the Son of man coming in the clouds of heaven with power and great glory."

Now follows the gathering of the elect. "And he shall send his angels with a great sound of a trumpet, and they shall gather together his elect from the four winds, from one end of heaven to the other" (vs. 31).

And what of the faithful servant? "He shall make him ruler" (vs. 47). "I will make thee ruler" (25: 14–30).

That He is to come in glory and that He is to be enthroned is clear from Matthew 25: 31—"When the Son of man shall come in his glory, and all the holy angels with him, then shall he sit upon the throne of his glory." Who is that Son of man? The King (vss. 34 and 40). So when He comes He first of all judges the living nations, and thus prepares the world for His millennial reign. Thus He puts down all rebellion and eliminates evil from His kingdom. Pilate it was who said of Him, "This is Jesus the King of the Jews" (Matt. 27: 37). Now at last He is King indeed.

Mark, in speaking of His coming, quotes Him as saying, "Ye shall see the Son of man sitting on the right hand of power, and coming in the clouds of heaven" (Mark 14: 62). Thus will He come when He comes to reign.

In Luke 22: 16–18, Jesus declares that He will

WHEN THE APOSTLES SAW THE KINGDOM

drink no more "of the fruit of the vine, until the kingdom of God shall come". So then He Himself most certainly believed in the kingdom. He knew it would come. But as He stated in Luke 17: 24–26, there must be first the suffering and then the glory. "Ought not Christ to have suffered these things, and to enter into his glory?" (Luke 24: 26).

WHAT ABOUT ISRAEL?

Now, Acts 2: 30:

"God . . . would raise up Christ to sit on his throne."

What throne? The throne of David. Who is to sit on it? Christ. Is David's throne in Heaven or on earth? It is on earth. Where then will Jesus reign? On earth. And to this agree all the words of the prophets.

Is God through with His people Israel? Has He cast them off forever? By no means. Harken now to the Apostle Paul as he speaks in Romans 11: 1, "I say then, Hath God cast away his people? God forbid. For I also am an Israelite, of the seed of Abraham, of the tribe of Benjamin. God hath not cast away his people which he foreknew." Yea, "all Israel shall be saved: as it is written, There shall come out of Sion the Deliverer, and shall turn away ungodliness from Jacob: For this is my covenant

WHEN THE KING COMES BACK

unto them, when I shall take away their sins" (Rom. 11: 26, 27).

<u>This prediction has yet to be fulfilled. Nationally Israel is to be restored and forgiven.</u> The Deliverer, or Redeemer (Isa. 59: 20, 21), will be Jesus Christ. He will regather, restore and convert His earthly people. Then they will be exalted. Their glory is still future. Nor will it be until their Messiah returns to Zion and becomes their Deliverer. That is God's plan for them and He will bring it to pass.

Now for Paul's great statement—1 Corinthians 15: 24–27. For one thousand years Jesus had reigned. "Then cometh the end, when he shall have delivered up the kingdom to God, even the Father; when he shall have put down all rule and all authority and power. For he must reign, till he hath put all enemies under his feet."

What a tremendous announcement! Here the Son delivers up the kingdom to the Father. All rulers, all worldly authority, all earthly powers, have at last been annihilated. There is no rebellion anywhere. All opposition has collapsed. It will be an unconditional surrender, the like of which mankind has never known before. But it will then be willing submission. And when that time comes, <u>Jesus Christ will hand the reins of government to God the Father, that God, the triune God, may be all in all</u>.

WHEN THE APOSTLES SAW THE KINGDOM

But what enemies are conquered? First of all, "death". Then, "all things". "The last enemy that shall be destroyed is death. For he hath put all things under his feet." No one yet has ever conquered death. It is the enemy of the entire human race. No one can escape it. Oh, the sorrow it brings! How men hate it! Yes, and how they fear it! But at long last it will be destroyed. "There shall be no more death, neither sorrow, nor crying, neither shall there be any more pain" (Rev. 21: 4).

Then too, "all things"—thrones, principalities and powers, angels and archangels, all the armies of evil, the whole universe—will then be conquered and brought into subjection to Jesus Christ. When that day comes, God alone will be supreme.

WHAT ABOUT THE CHURCH?

But what part will the Church have? Where do we come in? Look now at 2 Timothy 2: 12. It says: "If we suffer, we shall also reign with him." Oh, what a glorious prospect! "If we suffer." If we bear His reproach. If we endure persecution. If we are out and out for Jesus Christ. If we take our place with Him in this His day of rejection and humiliation. If we bear the cross. If we turn from the world that crucified Him and go without the camp. If we take sides with Him now. If we are

WHEN THE KING COMES BACK

faithful and loyal. If we follow Him here. If we do, we will reign with Him then.

<u>I am not satisfied to be saved. I want to return with Christ and share in His reign</u>. I long to see this old world when He takes over the reins of government. I want to be approved so that He can give me a position of authority in His kingdom. Those in His Church who have suffered will reign with Him for a thousand years. Will you be approved? Will you reign? Is He going to use you to help Him govern the world during the millennium? "If we suffer, we shall also reign." If we do not suffer, the inference is that we will not reign. What a solemn responsibility!

But will we be with Him? Listen to Jude 14— "Behold, the Lord cometh with ten thousands of his saints." So, He is coming back and He is bringing His saints with Him. You and I will be there. <u>First the Rapture, then the Revelation</u>. First we are caught up to Him; then we return with Him. For we are coming back as He is coming back. "We shall reign on the earth" (Rev. 5: 10).

[margin note: Time difference?]

HOW WILL HE COME?

See Revelation 1: 7:

"Behold, he cometh with clouds; and every eye shall see him, and they also which pierced him."

WHEN THE APOSTLES SAW THE KINGDOM

How will He come? With clouds. Who will see Him? All, but especially His own ancient people, those who cried, "Away with him. Crucify him." What will He look like when He comes to reign? See Revelation 1: 13-16:

"And in the midst of the seven candlesticks one like unto the Son of man, clothed with a garment down to the foot, and girt about the paps with a golden girdle. His head and his hairs were white like wool, as white as snow; and his eyes were as a flame of fire; And his feet like unto fine brass, as if they burned in a furnace; and his voice as the sound of many waters. And he had in his right hand seven stars: and out of his mouth went a sharp two-edged sword: and his countenance was as the sun shineth in his strength."

What majesty and glory! How different from when He came the first time!

Now comes the announcement of His universal dominion, the glorious fulfilment of Daniel's visions. "The kingdoms of this world are become the kingdoms of our Lord, and of his Christ; and he shall reign for ever and ever" (Rev. 11: 15). The hour has at last come to sing the Hallelujah Chorus. Jesus Christ is King. His kingdom dominates and overshadows all others. He is now the supreme Ruler. At last there is but one government, one King, and one kingdom, for He rules over all. He shall reign. Hallelujah!

WHEN THE KING COMES BACK

Note now what the four and twenty elders say: "Thou hast taken to thee thy great power, and hast reigned. And . . . thy wrath is come, and the time . . . that . . . thou . . . shouldest destroy them which destroy the earth." (Rev. 11: 17, 18). What a prediction! He reigns. He manifests His wrath. He destroys the rulers and nations that have brought desolation and destruction upon the earth.

Jesus Christ is now the supreme Ruler. No one can withstand Him. The nations with all their armament are powerless before Him. Rulers and potentates are destroyed. All opposition is put down. Rebels no longer rebel. His enemies at last lick the dust and all the world has been brought into subjection to Him.

KING OF KINGS AND LORD OF LORDS

This, then, is the "stone cut out without hands" (Dan. 2: 34, 35). Daniel saw Him. How John sees Him, and oh, what a description! Let us study it—Revelation 19: 11–16:

"And I saw heaven opened, and behold a white horse; and he that sat upon him was called Faithful and True, and in righteousness he doth judge and make war. His eyes were as a flame of fire, and on his head were many crowns; and he had a name

WHEN THE APOSTLES SAW THE KINGDOM

written, that no man knew, but he himself. And he was clothed with a vesture dipped in blood: and his name is called The Word of God.

"And the armies which were in heaven followed him upon white horses, clothed in fine linen, white and clean. And out of his mouth goeth a sharp sword, that with it he should smite the nations: and he shall rule them with a rod of iron: and he treadeth the winepress of the fierceness and wrath of Almighty God. And he hath on his vesture and on his thigh a name written, KING OF KINGS, AND LORD OF LORDS."

Yes, Jesus Christ is now King of kings and Lord of lords. And He rules the nations "with a rod of iron". No one rebels. No one makes war against Him. At long last He triumphs over all His foes. For, during His glorious reign, Satan, His archenemy, is imprisoned for the whole of the thousand year period (Rev. 20: 1–3).

Then reign the martyrs.

"And I saw thrones, and they sat upon them, and judgment was given unto them: and I saw the souls of them that were beheaded for the witness of Jesus, and for the word of God, and which had not worshipped the beast, neither his image, neither had received his mark upon their foreheads or in their hands; and they lived and reigned with Christ a thousand years."—Rev. 20: 4.

WHEN THE KING COMES BACK

Yes, they have their thrones. They reign with Christ. Who wouldn't be a martyr! What a glorious reward! "Behold, I come quickly," He exclaims, "and my reward is with me, to give every man according as his work shall be" (Rev. 22: 12). "Even so, come, Lord Jesus" (Rev. 22: 20).